For Richer,
For Poorer

For Richer, For Poorer

Shaping U.S.-Mexican Integration

Harry Browne
with **Beth Sims** *and* **Tom Barry**

No. 4 in The U.S.-Mexico Series

Resource Center Press
Albuquerque, New Mexico

and

Latin America Bureau
London

Resource Center Press
Box 4506 / Albuquerque, New Mexico 87196

ISBN: 0-911213-47-3 (U.S.)

Latin America Buruea
1 Amwell Street / London EC1R 1UL

The Latin America Bureau is an independent research and publishing organisation.
It works to broaden public understanding of issues of human rights and economic
justice in Latin America and the Caribbean.

First published in the UK in 1994 by Latin America Bureau (Research and Action)
Ltd, 1 Amwell Street, London EC1R 1UL

A catalogue record for this book is available from the British Library.

ISBN: 0 906156 90 4 (UK)

Trade distribution in the UK by: Central Books, 99 Wallis Road, London E9 5LN

Acknowledgments

We would like to thank the individuals and groups that are working hard in both countries to improve U.S.-Mexico relations and guide both countries along mutually beneficial paths of economic and social development. We are continually inspired by the openness, friendliness, and determination of the activists, academics, and community leaders who are every day experiencing the joys and challenges of U.S.-Mexico relations.

Many friends and colleagues contributed the footwork, insights, commentary, and analysis that were instrumental to writing this book. The staff at the Resource Center formed the foundation that allowed the book to take place. Especially important were the research assistance by Jerry Harvey, Rose Hansen, Laura Sheridan, and Steve Whitman; the administrative support offered by executive director Debra Preusch; and the editorial feedback and publications skills of production manager John Hawley. Our good friend Christine Jepson contributed much of her time and energy, without which we would still be pushing back deadlines.

Vital in detecting errors, correcting misconceptions, and offering important insights were the following experts who commented on parts of the manuscript and shared their information: Mark Anderson, Ron Blackwell, David Brooks, John Cavanagh, James Cypher, Ed Feigen, Paul Ganster, Steve Hecker, Thea Lee, Mary McGinn, Peter Morici, Wilson Peres, Christopher Whalen, and Matt Witt. We also gratefully acknowledge the financial support of the John D. and Catherine T. MacArthur Foundation, whose generous support made this book and the Resource Center's U.S.-Mexico project possible.

Contents

Economic Globalization Sets the Stage

Money and business are integrating North America. Economic forces—even more than transboundary migration, drug trafficking, or borderless ecosystems—are pulling Mexico and the United States together. In the process, the economic future of both countries is being shaped. On a broader scale, U.S.-Mexico integration illustrates the dramatic changes taking place in the world economy, as the economic systems of advanced and developing countries alike are being restructured to meet the needs of global traders and investors.

The technological, legal, and managerial innovations that have fostered economic globalization are obscure, but their effects are readily observable. Tens of thousands of jobs are relocated from one country to another each year, symbols of national identity like Columbia Pictures in the United States and Jaguar in Great Britain are bought up by foreign firms, and the products and logos of large corporations are increasingly familiar to people around the globe.

Globalization is tying people together in new ways, as can be seen in the city of Chihuahua in northern Mexico. Every weekday morning a couple of dozen company buses turn off the main avenue leading out of the city and into the parking lot of a Ford Motor Company engine plant. As the 540 first-shift employees report to work in the modern, concrete-and-glass facility, hundreds of cars fill an employee parking lot outside a much older Ford engine plant in Lima, Ohio, some 1,500 miles to the northeast. Separated by an international border, language, and an average age difference of thirty years, the two groups of workers are nevertheless part of the same corporate web. They produce for the same market with largely the same technology, answer to the same executives, and generate dividends for the same shareholders.

Thousands of similar corporate webs, ranging from very small local operations to the world's largest transnational corporations, link hundreds of thousands of workers in Mexico and the United States, as well as millions of consumers and shareholders. Although the movement of workers between Mexico and the United States remains heavily restricted, the countries have moved much closer together in the areas of trade and investment since the early 1980s.

Economic integration involves a reduction in the importance of national boundaries in the decisions of consumers, workers, and investors. This does not mean that national characteristics such as labor markets, infrastructure, and climate matter less. On the contrary, such characteristics become *more* important with integration because more people and corporations are freer to cross borders to take advantage of them.

A profound shift in the organization of manufacturing is to a large degree behind integration. Advances in telecommunications and transportation technology have made it possible to coordinate extremely complex manufacturing processes—from product design and investment financing to inventory management and marketing—in several countries simultaneously. Managers have "rationalized" their operations and reduced costs by splitting up portions of their production chains and relocating the various links to countries with lower labor costs, more competitive suppliers, cheaper natural resources, or more favorable government policies.

The production of televisions by the Japanese electronics giant Hitachi illustrates the process of globalization.[1] First, Hitachi marketers in the United States estimate how many of which models their distributors will need in six weeks. Based on this information, orders go out to a Singaporean subcontractor, who manufactures the specified transistors and ships them to a Malaysian circuit board assembler. From Malaysia the circuit boards travel to Taiwan, where workers assemble controller chassis, again following Hitachi's product mix instructions. With two weeks to go other components are ordered from Hitachi affiliates in Japan. A week later the chassis and other parts arrive in Tijuana, where they are joined by picture tubes and deflection yokes made by a Dutch company in the United States. Mexican workers assemble wood and plastic panels shipped from the United States, attach the electronic innards, and run the televisions through a battery of quality control tests. Workers then package the TVs and ship them to the United States with two or three days to spare.

The replacement of traditional, locally based manufacturing with international assembly lines like Hitachi's is commonly termed the globalization of production. Although corporations in search of markets and workers are the main actors in the process of integration, their technological advances and transnational production networks alone do not explain globalization. Governments play a critical role in establishing the rules under which corporations act. A legal framework conducive to foreign investment, low barriers to trade, an efficient international financial system, and a stable, probusiness political atmosphere are also crucial elements. Throughout the post-World War II era the United States has worked to put these elements into place, largely by pushing other countries to adopt open trade and investment policies.

In 1990 the international free market agenda took center stage in North America when Mexican President Carlos Salinas de Gortari and U.S. President George Bush announced they would negotiate a North American Free Trade Agreement (NAFTA). Later enlarged to include Canada, the proposal envisioned a continent without tariffs, quotas, or investment restrictions.

The proposal for NAFTA was an attempt to guide economic integration on a regional basis, but regional integration has global implications. The economic relationship developing across the Rio Grande bridges an enormous gap in economic development and living standards and represents a prototype for the rapidly changing roles played by the post-industrial North and the industrializing South in the global economy.[2] North America is a crucible in which advanced technology, subsistence farming, global finance capital, massive underemployment, and sharply contrasting legal and political systems are being mixed for the first time. How policy makers and social forces shape the process of integration and what the results of integration are will help define the development strategies of poor countries, the competitive strategies of wealthier ones, and the ability of all nations and citizens to influence their own destinies.

The United States and Mexico appeared to cement the process of economic integration in December 1992 with the signing of NAFTA. But mounting evidence in both countries pointed to problems with their governments' economic strategies. Many observers in both countries questioned the management of North American integration and advocated new responses to the challenges of globalization.

The United States in the Global Economy

The United States pushed the international economy to open up after World War II, making the General Agreement on Tariffs and Trade (GATT) one of the centerpieces of its effort. As the dominant force in the capitalist world the United States was largely able to get its way. Negotiations under GATT resulted in a steady lowering of trade barriers, and U.S. manufacturers saw a widening global market for their goods.

In the 1960s the more visionary corporate managers saw that freer trade flows meant access not just to consumer markets but also to vast labor markets. Led by the electronics and apparel industries, these managers set up labor-intensive facilities in Asia, the Caribbean, and Mexico. In most cases the shift to new, globally oriented plants enabled corporations to weaken labor unions, cut wage costs, and increase managerial control over the organization of work. As globalization progressed both workers and governments found themselves in more direct international competition for a limited pool of capital and technology.

Few policy makers noticed these effects as long as the U.S. economy was growing steadily. But the recessions of the 1970s began to draw attention to the fact that U.S. corporations were sending jobs abroad at the same time that employment opportunities at home were becoming scarcer. And the huge trade deficit that the United States racked up in the 1980s spotlighted trade policies as a possible source of declining economic security.

By the late 1980s millions of workers who had formed the backbone of the middle class had been thrown out of work by plant shutdowns. Government studies indicated that more than one-half of all "displaced" workers were still unemployed six months after being laid off. Even among workers who succeeded in regaining employment, more had moved down the pay scale in taking their new positions than had moved up. On average, displaced workers suffered real earnings losses of 10 percent to 15 percent.[3]

Laid-off workers were not the only ones seeing their salaries drop. New entrants to the work force competed with those experienced workers whose jobs had been eliminated. And although the economy was generating new jobs, few of these paid a family wage. From 1979 to 1987, 21.2 million more jobs were created than had been lost. But over half of the new positions paid less than the poverty line for a family of four—$13,400 per year—and only one out of thirteen paid over the median annual salary of $26,800.[4] Millions of workers were able to keep their jobs only by agreeing to employers' demands for wage and benefit cuts or, in nonunion settings, by implicitly accepting them. These trends have meant more work and less pay for the average worker, a widening income gap between the top 20 percent of households and everyone else, and fewer opportunities for anyone without postsecondary education.[5]

Two strains of thought developed in the United States about how to respond to these economic trends. In one camp are neo-liberals, who believe that the fall in workers' wages, the widening income gap, and the growing trade deficit are the natural results of a globalizing international economy. Tinkering with market forces will only make things worse, they argue, and in the long term the trade deficit will shrink and employment and wages will grow again. Neoliberals point to the massive inflow of foreign capital in the 1980s as evidence of the soundness of the U.S. econ-omy.[6] Investors would be unlikely to buy assets in dollars, they reason, if the country were headed downhill. From this perspective the best policy option is to continue to open the U.S. economy and to encourage other countries to follow the U.S. lead.[7]

A second strain of policy thought which could be called *real-economik* began to challenge the neoliberal position during the 1980s. According to this view the United States' reliance on the free market places it at a competitive disadvantage vis-à-vis its trading partners, who play by different rules. In east Asia and western Europe national governments have developed industrial policies that target strategic economic sectors ranging from steel production and ship building to the semiconductor and aerospace industries. They have also coordinated and subsidized large-scale worker-training programs. With government support, businesses in targeted industries are able to win market share from U.S.-based firms, both abroad and in the United States. The trade deficit is exhibit number one for this position. And the inflow of foreign capital, far from being a good sign, represents a huge mortgage taken out by U.S. consumers for which future genera-tions will pay dearly.[8]

Academics and policy makers in the *realeconomik* camp pushed the United States to adopt an industrial policy to improve the country's international competitiveness. Many of them admitted that this was a second-best solution to the United States' international economic problems: Ideally other countries would change their systems by reducing their governments' economic role and by dropping barriers to foreign trade and investment. But attempting to convince them to do so by example and through gentle persuasion was ineffective, especially since industrial policies had served their business interests well over the previous decades. Instead, they concluded, the United States should play by their rules, raise barriers to some imports, and target specific industries for government support. In addition, most proponents of an industrial policy include some form of a national worker-training program in their proposals.

The idea of enhancing U.S. competitiveness raises far more questions than it answers. What does competitiveness mean—is it profits, jobs, quality of life, a trade surplus, or something else? Where does it come from? What factors lead an investor to choose one site over another? Should there be rules for the ways countries seek competitive advantages, such as a ban on slave labor or a cap on government subsidies? If so, how should they be determined and enforced?

For neoliberals, U.S.-Mexican economic relations provide an important part of the answer to these questions. The United States will stay competitive if its companies stay competitive, and its companies can do that by transferring certain jobs to Mexico. The government should facilitate production sharing by removing obstacles to trade and investment. But to those in the industrial policy camp, this strategy sounds like keeping the ship and crew afloat by ordering passengers to jump overboard. Instead of making it easier for companies to move outside the United States, they argue, the government should adopt a national economic strategy, help businesses upgrade their technology and worker-training programs, fight back against unfair competition, and work to create international social standards.

Although neoliberals and industrial policy advocates disagree on the proper economic role for government, both focus on enhancing the international competitiveness of U.S.-based corporations.[9] A third, considerably smaller strain of thought gained strength during the debate over NAFTA in the early 1990s but posed little challenge to the two dominant perspectives. Unlike the neoliberal and *realeconomik* perspectives, this view rejects unfettered capitalism as the primary basis for domestic or international policy. Advocates of this position are concerned that an industrial policy would tilt the already skewed balance of economic and political power even further toward the corporate elite and away from workers, small businesses, and grassroots activists. These progressives argue that international economic agreements should cover much more than trade and investment issues. Environmental standards, labor rights, consumer protection, and the ability of nations to regulate capital are all affected by institutions like GATT and need to be included in negotiations, they say.

Until the election of Bill Clinton in 1992 the neoliberal position held sway in Washington. The treatment prescribed by the Reagan and Bush administrations for the nation's economic malaise was in effect to take more of the same. Domestically, the government refused to consider an industrial policy and in fact moved in the other direction by rescinding the investment tax credit, deregulating a number of industries, and defanging enforcement agencies like the Occupational Safety and Health Administration and the Environmental Protection Agency. Internationally, the *realeconomik* camp had slightly more success, winning official recognition—first by Congress and then by the Office of the U.S. Trade Representative—that the international economic "playing field" was uneven and often sloped against U.S. corporations.

But, with the exception of some subsidy and export-promotion programs, the Reagan and Bush administrations rejected the "if you can't persuade 'em, fight 'em on their own terms" advice of industrial policy advocates. Instead they pursued a grand vision of global economic policy convergence based on neoliberalism. Reagan proposed the first element in this strategy—a free trade zone "from the Yukon to the Yucatán"—as a presidential candidate in 1980. But with no immediate takers, he had to settle for a much more modest program: the Caribbean Basin Initiative (CBI). Proposed in 1981 and in place by 1983, CBI consisted of a combination of aid and trade incentives aimed at the politically sensitive and economically troubled regions of Central America and the Caribbean. To participate in CBI, countries had to adopt laws protecting the rights of foreign investors.

The initiative was designed to increase economic ties between the United States and CBI participants and to encourage the latter to follow a development path well within the bounds of international capitalism. Although CBI itself did not oblige participating countries to open their domestic markets to imports, the Reagan administration pursued this objective by conditioning much of its economic assistance on import liberalization by recipient countries. The United States applied added pressure for lower trade barriers in the Third World through its central role in renegotiating developing countries' international debts and its influence in the International Monetary Fund and the World Bank.

To move toward the broader global vision, Reagan pushed for a broadening and deepening of GATT, proposing an eighth round of talks in 1982. Four years later, following considerable U.S. efforts, talks began in Uruguay. United States negotiators set an ambitious goal for what is called the Uruguay Round: the inclusion of services and agricultural products under GATT's umbrella. Both sectors were excluded from the original GATT mandate because virtually all nations—the United States included—sought to protect their domestic financial and food systems. But the U.S. position shifted as the country's manufacturing industries lost their competitive advantage and as U.S. agribusinesses and financial institutions grew stronger. Trade officials expected that opening up European, Asian, and Latin American markets to U.S. farmers, insurance companies, and banks would go a long way toward correcting the country's huge trade deficit.

With such an ambitious agenda, the Uruguay Round dragged on for years. While GATT remained the top priority for U.S. negotiators, the slow going prompted three regional efforts at trade and investment accords: the U.S.-Canada free trade agreement, signed in 1988; the Enterprise for the Americas Initiative, launched by President Bush in 1990; and NAFTA. The Reagan and Bush administrations advanced these regional proposals with several economic objectives in mind.[10]

The first such objective was to increase the rate of U.S. economic growth, even if only slightly, through free trade and broader investment options. Free traders saw opportunities looking both north and south. Canada is the country's leading trade partner, forms a crucial part of the U.S. automobile-manufacturing base, and has resources—mainly oil and water—of great potential interest to the United States. Mexico ranks third as a trade partner, but with high import barriers in key areas, an agreement with Mexico could boost U.S. exports significantly. At least as important in Mexico's case was the liberalization of investment restrictions in a number of sectors previously off limits to foreigners.

The second objective behind the regional proposals was the Bush administration's hope that North American free trade would speed the GATT process by setting precedents for trade and investment provisions. The U.S.-Canada accord and NAFTA both dealt with the unglamorous but very important subject of intellectual property rights—the protection of trademarks, copyrights, and patents—as well as liberalization of the financial services and agricultural sectors. All of these areas were central to the Uruguay Round.

The United States also looked to regional agreements to strengthen its negotiating position within GATT. NAFTA and the proposed Enterprise for the Americas Initiative—George Bush's plan to unite the hemisphere in a series of bilateral and multilateral free trade agreements—improved the United States' "fallback" position. That is, they reduced the cost to the United States of failing to sign a GATT deal by laying the foundation for a smaller but still significant liberalized trade and investment region.[11] By 1992 the United States had signed sixteen "framework" agreements—a preliminary step to trade negotiations—involving thirty-one countries in the hemisphere. This lent credibility to U.S. statements that it would pull out of the Uruguay Round if its bottom-line offer was not accepted.

With a Democrat in the White House for the first time in twelve years, it is unclear to what extent the United States will continue to insist on trade agreements that reflect the neoliberal ideology. During his presidential campaign Bill Clinton placed himself within the *realeconomik* camp, stating that he supported free trade in principle, but cautioning that "if they won't play by our rules, we'll play by theirs."[12]

Mexico in the Global Economy

As the globalization of production hollowed out the manufacturing base of many economically advanced countries, it was also transforming many less developed countries. In a handful of Asian and Latin American nations, including Mexico, the foreign investment binge that was a central part of globalization gave birth to modern, export-oriented industrial sectors.

The east Asian countries—in particular Taiwan, South Korea, and Singapore—linked their economies to international markets and leveraged foreign investment into economic growth, trade surpluses, and slowly rising wages. In these cases strong central governments repressed organized labor, adopted stable, probusiness foreign investment policies, provided low-cost, well-trained work forces, and carved out distinct economic niches for themselves through national development strategies.[13] Neither Mexico nor other Latin American newly industrializing countries (NICs) like Brazil, Colombia, and Argentina were able to stimulate growth through foreign investment as had South Korea, Taiwan, and Singapore. Governments in both sets of NICs intervened heavily in their national economies, but whereas the east Asian countries shifted to an export-oriented strategy in the 1960s, their Latin American counterparts followed more inward-looking policies until the 1980s.[14]

The experiences of the east Asian "tigers" provided evidence that participation in the international economy could promote capitalist development, given appropriate government policies. This evidence ran counter to the prevalent view of underdevelopment in Latin America and elsewhere, called dependency theory. Dependency theory held that developing countries could not hope to catch up to the North through trade and foreign investment. Once linked economically, development in the South would depend on and be secondary to the consumer needs and investment patterns of the North. Dependency theorists also argued that the value of advanced Northern products would constantly increase relative to the value of Southern goods and that foreign investment would only lead to capital outflow through profit repatriation and other means. By undermining a central premise of dependency theory, east Asia's experience with globalization had an indirect political impact felt throughout the developing world.[15]

For reasons of history and internal political structures, nearly all Latin American countries—even those in which foreign investment had built export-oriented manufacturing sectors—resisted globalization's pull to join the world economy until the 1980s. Instead they pursued an inward-looking development strategy called import-substituting industrialization (ISI). As its name suggests, the goal of ISI was to develop a strong industrial base by encouraging the domestic production of previously imported goods.

Rooted in the region's disastrous experience with international markets in the Great Depression of the 1930s, ISI was also intended to minimize dependence on international trade and foreign investment.[16]

Mexico was one of the most vigorous and successful exponents of ISI. Starting in the 1920s and accelerating after World War II, Mexico raised tariffs and imposed other barriers to imports, assigning the highest duties to those goods that economic planners felt would be easiest to produce domestically—such as apparel, footwear, and bottled beverages.

In some areas domestic capitalists did not have the know-how to replace imports, so the government looked to transnational corporations (TNCs) for help. Foreign corporations were attracted to Mexico because its protected market offered high prices and little competition, and it gave them a chance to squeeze additional profit out of technology they had already developed. Mexico hoped that TNCs would transfer their advanced technology and managerial techniques to Mexican workers and managers, and that they would spark the development of local supplier industries.

But Mexican decision makers were also deeply distrustful of foreign corporations. Multinational firms could not be counted on to set production targets and marketing strategies that would best serve Mexico's development goals. And they could end up siphoning large amounts of foreign exchange out of the country through profit remittances and royalty payments to their parent firms. To reduce reliance on TNCs over the long term, the country's strategy called for the "Mexicanization" of foreign firms. According to this plan, when domestic industrialists had learned enough and were ready to take over, the government would force TNCs to sell them at least a majority interest in their operations.

Mexico's distrust of foreign corporations—which was echoed throughout the Third World—stemmed in large part from the country's experience with foreign investors in a previous period: the thirty-five-year rule of General Porfirio Díaz from 1876 to 1910. The economy during the *porfiriato*, as the General's reign is known, provides a textbook case of dependent development. Díaz relied on foreign capitalists to improve the country's physical and financial infrastructure. Railroads, mines, oil wells, banks, and large-scale agriculture flourished during the *porfiriato*, but they were thoroughly dominated by foreign firms, mostly from the

United States.[17] Díaz and his bureaucrats benefited richly from the gratitude of foreign companies, but the rest of the country was left out of the game. Most of the railroads, for example, served only to transport foreign-owned ores or crops to foreign-controlled ports for shipment abroad. Frustrated with foreign economic domination and the regime's corruption and aided by the discontent of peasants and workers, a collection of military, business, and middle-class leaders forced Díaz into exile in 1911 and took control of the government. The constitution they adopted in 1917 launched Mexico on a very different development path. Mexico became a leader among developing countries in advocating a strong economic role for the state, favoring domestic capitalists over foreign, and seeking maximum autonomy from the world economy.

Fulfilling the constitutional goal of subordinating foreign investors to national interests required a series of executive or legislative measures that have been variously enforced. The most dramatic decree came in 1938, when President Lázaro Cárdenas announced the expropriation of all foreign oil firms.[18] By the time Cárdenas left office in 1940, foreign capital contributed only 15 percent of total investment in Mexico's economy, down from 66 percent in the first decade of the 1900s.

The policy of Mexicanization, combined with booming domestic investment, greatly reduced Mexico's overall reliance on TNCs. In the 1950s, foreign capital averaged around 10 percent of total investment, in the 1960s it was around 5 percent, and in the 1970s less than 3 percent of total investment each year came from abroad. But in several of the fastest-growing industries—automobiles, pharmaceuticals, and later, computers—multinational corporations maintained an overwhelmingly dominant position.

Import-substituting industrialization also succeeded in its initial goals of reducing imports and promoting domestic manufacturing. From 1939 to 1969 imports fell rapidly as a proportion of total Mexican demand and the economy grew at the very impressive average annual rate of 6 percent from 1940 to 1975.[19] Mexico was a model for other countries that employed the ISI strategy.

In the 1970s, however, what had come to be known as the Mexican miracle began to peter out. Although imports had fallen relative to the size the country's economy, they were growing in absolute terms. Mexico still depended on imports to supply the capital goods, special materials, and technologies demanded by industry. And it had failed to develop more than a few industries (cement, glass, and steel) capable of penetrating export markets. Mexico's inability to feed itself exacerbated the problem. In 1970 Mexico exported 3.5 times as much food as it imported, but by 1980 food imports exceeded exports by 74 percent.

With imports growing faster than exports, Mexico entered a period of economic instability beginning in the mid-1970s in which it became increasingly dependent on oil revenue and foreign loans. In 1982 Mexico got hit by a double-whammy: Oil prices sank and interest rates skyrocketed. The incoming administration of President Miguel de la Madrid had two basic choices: unilaterally alter the terms of debt repayment or accept the limited relief and economic prescriptions offered by the United States, Japan, and the International Monetary Fund. De la Madrid and others in Mexico's government understood that the world economy was moving toward integration, and they knew that economic modernization would require foreign capital and know-how. They opted to cooperate with their creditors.[20]

Far from renouncing the debt, de la Madrid fashioned a strategy to become Latin America's "model debtor." His administration kept interest payments current and even pressured other debtor nations to come to terms with their creditors rather than declaring debt moratoriums. The president reasoned that staking out this position would put Mexico first in line for a debt relief package, while quickly enhancing the country's image in the eyes of foreign investors.[21]

At the same time, Mexico did a U-turn in economic policy, dropping ISI and Mexicanization and adopting a neoliberal strategy. Neoliberalism holds that reducing the size of the government and removing all barriers to free market activities will produce economic growth that eventually will benefit everyone. Intent on attracting foreign investment and promoting exports, de la Madrid slashed government spending and rapidly devalued the *peso*, giving investors more for their dollars and making exports cheaper. To alter the structure of the domestic economy he began to sell off some of the more than 2,000 government-owned businesses. These policy shifts responded to the wishes of the IMF and the United States, but they also reflected the economic orientation of de la Madrid and most of his advisors.

Mexico demonstrated the depth of its changes in 1986 when it signed on to the General Agreement on Tariffs and Trade. De la Madrid cut tariffs far faster than the schedule GATT required, winning considerable acclaim from conservative foreign economists. The strategy wreaked havoc on the country's formerly protected manufacturers, however, since they had neither the resources nor the time to adjust to powerful international competitors.

It took seven years of economic stagnation and a devastating decline in the living standards of the large majority of Mexicans for the new approach to achieve its objective of regaining creditworthiness. In 1989, under the new government of President Carlos Salinas, Mexico signed a debt-reduction deal with representatives of private international lenders. The country was again able to float bonds on international markets, and that same year Salinas opened up Mexico's stock market to foreign participation.

The debt deal, the commitment of Mexico's leaders to liberalization, and the potential for unlimited access to the U.S. market ignited euphoria in international business circles. Supporters of the neoliberal program hailed Salinas as a hero and pointed to Mexico's renewed economic growth even as the global economy slipped into recession.

But even if neoliberalism leads to sustained economic growth—and the jury is out on that question—it is apparent that a very large portion of Mexico's population will be left out of these gains. Privatization, cuts in government programs, wage repression, and currency devaluations widened the already large gap between rich and poor in Mexican society. Real wages dropped by as much as 40 percent from 1981 to 1992, and the ranks of the un- or underemployed expanded rapidly. Workers' share of aggregate personal income declined from 36 percent in the mid-1970s to 25 percent in 1988, and 23 percent in 1992.[22] The vast gulf between the wealthiest ten percent of Mexicans and the nearly 50 percent who live below the poverty line grew vaster during the 1980s.[23] With the government cutting social programs for urban and rural populations alike, there is little reason to foresee the income gap closing.

Private sector economic control also grew increasingly concentrated from 1982 on. The privatization process launched in 1985 and rapidly accelerated by the Salinas administration served mainly to pass businesses from government hands to the control of Mexico's wealthy elite, although on occasion foreign partners were included. The country's opening to imports also contributed to this trend. Low-cost and high-quality foreign goods forced a great number of small- and mid-size Mexican firms to declare bankruptcy or to drop production activities and focus on distributing imported products. As a result, the twenty-five largest companies—including two owned by the government—accounted for 47.1 percent of Mexico's gross domestic product by the end of 1991.[24] This sort of economic concentration does not bode well for Mexican consumers or for the nation's political stability.

Other Latin American leaders take great interest in the social effects of Mexico's policy shift. Although these leaders have been influenced by east Asia's development, Mexico's history and society make its experience more relevant to the Americas. The country's neoliberal experiment has become the continent's experiment as other nations struggle to come to terms with the changing global economy. Chile and Bolivia had adopted strict neoliberal policies prior to Mexico, but Mexico held special importance: Not only was it Latin America's second largest economy, it had also been a leading practitioner of inward-looking development.[25]

To Latin American leaders, Mexico's economic growth was good but hardly awe-inspiring: Its per capita gross domestic product grew by 1.3 percent in 1989, 2.4 percent in 1990, 1.5 percent in 1991, and 0.4 percent in 1992.[26] These figures did not seem to justify the threat to domestic capitalists of extensive trade liberalization, or the loss of national economic control entailed in dropping foreign investment restrictions and cutting back on government subsidies and other programs.

Furthermore, it is unlikely that other Latin American nations could repeat even Mexico's mediocre growth figures simply by following its strategy. In many ways Mexico reaped the benefits of being a model economic "reformer." A desire to reward Mexico has meant that in each year since President Salinas took office Mexico has been ranked first in the world in total nonpoverty lending by the World Bank. In 1992 Mexico became the World Bank's largest recipient, with more than $12 billion in outstanding loans. Nearly 40 percent of all World Bank loans to Latin American nations went to Mexico from 1989 to 1991.[27] The U.S. Export-Import Bank has also supported Mexico's economic program, making more than half of its Latin American loans to that country.[28]

Political factors provide another reason to hesitate to go farther down the neoliberal path. Apart from the negative impact of foreign competition on a large part of the politically influential business sector, Latin American leaders fear that holding down wages, devaluing currencies, cutting government subsidies, and allowing foreign corporations to operate with few restrictions could spark popular unrest. It is not necessarily that these leaders have the interests of the poor at heart—in most cases their history indicates otherwise—but they do have an interest in maintaining social peace. This is especially true for the many governments that are attempting to consolidate fragile electoral democracies after years of harsh military rule. Few nations in the region have the efficient mechanisms of state social control that Mexico has and that Chile had during its shift to neoliberalism.

Mexico's neighbors to the southeast are watching the country closely not just to pick up clues for their own economic policy making but also because Mexico represents a competitive threat to their economies. Many of Mexico's exports compete directly with those of Caribbean and Central and South American countries. These include agricultural products such as coffee, sugar, cattle, fruits, and vegetables, and manufactures like apparel and steel. Just as important, all developing nations are in competition for international investment capital, especially as they start to look to exports as an engine of growth. As Mexico makes it easier for multinational corporations to operate there, other countries are pressured to respond in kind. The stock markets of Argentina, Brazil, Chile, and Venezuela have either put in place or announced policies similar to Mexico's opening to foreign stock investors.

It was largely to enhance Mexico's competitive position both in exporting and attracting investment that Salinas announced in 1990 that he would seek a free trade agreement with the United States. A successful accord would ensure Mexican products access to the hemisphere's dominant market. This assured access would increase the country's attractiveness to foreign investors who wanted to export to the United States. An accord would also encourage investors by increasing the likelihood that future Mexican administrations would adhere to free-market policies. Successor administrations would have the option of backing out of an agreement, but the costs of doing so—a loss of international credibility and investor confidence—would be much higher than if such policies were not part of an international agreement.

The free trade agreement that presidents Bush and Salinas signed in 1992—together with Canadian Prime Minister Brian Mulroney—represents an acceptance and reinforcement of the existing international economic system. Neither administration took an interest in exploring the possibilities for regulating the flows of goods and capital in ways that might benefit those workers, peasants, and others who were already losing out under neoliberalism (although both accepted the "need" to restrict the flow of human beings). Nor did they consider ways to slow or reverse the shift of economic power from workers, citizens, and governments to corporations.

But other social sectors have taken a great interest in just these questions, prompted by the spreading human and social costs of globalization and restructuring. From labor unions representing blue- and pink-collar workers and low-income community-organizing projects to environmental and consumer groups supported largely by wealthier professionals, nongovernmental organizations are exploring the possible effects of integration and searching for and promoting alternatives.

The globalization of production is pushing free trade in North America, but it is more than a case of regional economic integration; the evolving free trade relationship between the United States and Mexico foreshadows the future of North-South relations in general. This process of integration of the U.S. and Mexican economies is one of joining countries with vastly different standards of living and highly disparate economic bases. It is just such North-South integration that is the wave of the future, and shaping it for maximum social benefit is the challenge facing all parties involved. What comes out of North American integration will set a critical precedent—not just for this hemisphere but for the entire world.

Chapter 1

Ties that Bind

Even before Mexico and the United States began the NAFTA negotiations, the economic ties that bind the two neighbors were tightening. Mexico's drive to liberalize its economy together with global market pressures and Washington's own drive to open up the hemisphere to U.S. trade and investment have led to a sharp expansion of economic relations between the two nations since the early 1980s. Total binational trade nearly tripled between 1983 and 1992, and the value of authorized U.S. direct investment in Mexico grew even faster.[29]

Automobiles and auto parts led the trade boom, followed by electrical equipment and machinery, telecommunications equipment, and computers. All told, manufactured goods constitute more than 80 percent of U.S. exports to and about 70 percent of U.S. imports from Mexico. The mostly foreign-owned, export-oriented assembly plants known as maquiladoras account for roughly one-third of the trade in manufactures. Mineral fuels—chiefly petroleum—and agricultural products are also significant elements of U.S.-Mexico commerce, contributing 9 percent and 7 percent, respectively, to total trade.[30]

Both countries have greeted the expanding trade and investment connections enthusiastically. But the larger U.S. economy, the globe-trotting character of U.S. corporations, and the greater demand for U.S. goods mean that binational business is hardly a relationship between equals. For the most part, U.S.-Mexico trade and investment are characterized by asymmetry. Although both countries are eager to strengthen economic ties, Mexico is much more dependent on the binational commercial relationship for its economic and political stability.

The United States accounts for more than 70 percent of Mexico's exports and imports and provides some 63 percent of the country's foreign investment. In contrast, Mexico accounts for only 7 percent of total U.S. trade, and a minuscule amount of foreign direct investment in the United States.[31] Mexican exports to the United States add around 13 percent to its gross domestic product; U.S. exports to Mexico barely register above the noise of statistical error at one-half of 1 percent of U.S. GDP. Only in the binational trade balance have the two countries achieved a degree of parity. During most of the 1980s Mexico enjoyed commercial surpluses with the United States. In 1991, however, Mexico started importing from the United States more than it was exporting there, and by 1992 Mexico's trade deficit with the United States had reached $4.7 billion. Whether such deficits persist depends largely on Mexico's exchange-rate policy and the level of foreign investment in the country.

The economic asymmetry of the U.S.-Mexico relationship is also seen on other fronts. Mexico's large external debt has given Washington and U.S. bankers leverage over its economic policies, and the preponderant influence of the United States in such multilateral lenders as the World Bank and the International Monetary Fund also skews the economic relations between the two nations. Also a factor is the array of U.S. agencies—from the promotional and informational services of the Commerce Department and the U.S. Foreign Agricultural Service to the financial services offered by U.S. Eximbank—that support the aggressive expansion of U.S. trade and investment in Mexico.

The more powerful position of the United States along with Mexico's more pressing need to maintain good relations with its northern neighbor place Mexico in a weak and vulnerable position in trade negotiations. Washington has repeatedly taken advantage of the asymmetric partnership to gain Mexican cooperation with U.S. priorities. Because of Mexico's almost desperate need to expand exports to the United States, it has quickly caved in to most U.S. trade demands. Such was the case in 1990, when U.S. Trade Representative Carla Hills placed Mexico on the "Priority Watch List" of trading partners whose policies the USTR considers unfairly biased against U.S. companies. Washington's threat of withdrawing preferential tariff treatment affecting $220 million of Mexican chemical industry exports persuaded Mexico to drastically rewrite its laws on intellectual property rights—the protection of trademarks, patents, and copyrights—even before NAFTA was negotiated.

The United States has also bullied Mexico with its antidumping and countervailing duties laws. From leather apparel and ceramic tile in 1980 to cement and steel in the early 1990s, the ability of Mexican exporters to reach the U.S. market has been subject to the determinations of the U.S. Treasury Department and International Trade Commission. These agencies have often slapped Mexican exporters with duties intended to compensate for—or "countervail"—alleged advantages gained by selling products below "fair market value" or by receiving "unfair" government subsidies. But in many cases the duties have been politically motivated, intended to satisfy key domestic interest groups or to send messages to the Mexican government.[32]

Even with a free trade agreement in place, such power politics in international trade is likely to continue given Mexico's deepening dependence on U.S. trade and investment and its fear of endangering smooth commercial relations with the United States. Such is the nature of business between unequal partners.

The Changing Face of Mexico

Accelerating U.S.-Mexico trade and investment flows alter more than the figures on international balance sheets. Sparked by Mexico's dramatic economic restructuring and liberalization, the expanded relationship with U.S. traders and investors is the most prominent sign of how the whole character of Mexico is changing. As U.S. investment and goods increase their penetration of Mexico, urban and rural residents are adopting new spending and work patterns. Accentuating the impact of the broadened commercial ties is the steady advance of U.S. culture.

The two- or three-hour lunch break is rapidly losing ground to the quick-bite-to-eat approach, especially for urban professionals. McDonald's, Kentucky Fried Chicken, Pizza Hut, and a multitude of other U.S.-owned fast-food outlets—even Taco Bell—are sprouting up all over Mexico to meet the demand caused by changing eating habits. Hundreds of foreign franchises are slicing deeply into family-owned food businesses, in effect replacing small entrepreneurs with hourly workers.

The shopping mall, invented and perfected in the United States, is fast becoming a part of Mexican cultural life—at least for the one-third or so of the population able to buy more than bare necessities. The malls seek to create a first world look—one even features an ice-skating rink—making U.S. retailers like Sears, J.C. Penney, and Dillard's increasingly attractive to developers of commercial property. Seeking U.S. marketing experience and inventory technology, established Mexican retailers are eagerly pursuing joint ventures with U.S. chains, including Wal-Mart and Price Club. Although these huge, relatively low-margin operations please their affluent customers, they pose a tremendous challenge to the small, locally owned shops that conduct 70 percent of Mexico's retail business. One business handbook predicts that the "superstore" invasion could cut that share to 40 percent by the year 2000.[33]

Advertising, especially on television, is a primary force in the mixing of U.S. values with Mexican culture. The new U.S. owners or co-owners of Mexican firms use marketing techniques familiar to any U.S. consumer in their promotional campaigns and often use the same ad agencies in Mexico and the United States. Eight of the top ten advertising firms in Mexico are foreign-owned.

No economic sector remains untouched by the penetration of U.S. goods and investment. Most evident has been the wide range of U.S. manufactures and processed foods now offered by Mexico's retail sector. Even before high-powered U.S. retailers began to move into the Mexican market, U.S.-made goods were putting Mexican manufacturers on the defensive—or, in many cases, out of business. Since Mexico began lowering its trade barriers after joining GATT in 1986, the quantity and variety of U.S.-made goods available to the Mexican consumer have mushroomed. Consumer goods accounted for only 7 percent of all Mexican imports from 1983 to 1987, but by 1990 they had grown to represent 17 percent of all imports.[34] Manufacturers of shoes, textiles, toys, and consumer electronics lead the long list of Mexican industries that formerly operated behind strong trade barriers and are now facing ruin.

In the export-oriented manufacturing sector only a few Mexican industries operate at the levels of scale and efficiency required to compete in the U.S. market. Thanks to the protectionist, state-directed policies that Mexican economic planners now reject, several private conglomerates did emerge in the 1960s and 1970s that have the financial resources to withstand the challenge of transnational corporations. In such areas as cement, beer, and glass, these business groups are even putting U.S. and European firms on the defensive with their marketing and investment strategies.

For the most part, however, nonpetroleum export-oriented manufacturing is controlled by foreign, mainly U.S., corporations. This U.S. presence is especially prominent in the maquiladora assembly sector. With their low wages and close integration into the U.S. market, maquiladoras represent a preview of the kind of manufacturing partnership that NAFTA may bring.

But the automotive sector is perhaps even more important as an indicator of the new economic relationship developing between the United States and Mexico. In the 1970s U.S. car manufacturers began shifting aspects of their operations—particularly labor-intensive parts assembly—to maquiladoras in Mexico. Although maquila assembly remains an important part of the Mexico-based automotive industry, since the early 1980s all five car manufacturers in Mexico have also established major manufacturing facilities that produce engines and in some cases entire vehicles, using the most advanced technology and production systems. As U.S. car companies find that they can achieve equal or higher levels of efficiency and quality in Mexico at much lower labor costs, more of their operations are being shut down in the United States and reestablished in places like Hermosillo and Chihuahua.

The automotive industry is not alone in finding that Mexico is suitable not only for low-skill, labor-intensive manufacturing but also for more skilled production processes involving robotics, laser technology, and real-time manufacturing control systems. Kodak film, IBM computers, and Whirlpool appliances are among the many products being manufactured, not just assembled, in Guadalajara, Monterrey, and other Mexican cities.

Rural residents lack the buying power to attract multinational retailers or franchisees, but they are keenly aware of Mexico's opening to the international economy. No group has been hit as hard by the lifting of import barriers as small farmers. Having suffered decades of neglect and political manipulation by the ruling party, they are incapable of competing with the world's most efficient farmers just to their north. Farmers in the United States and Canada not only use sophisticated growing and harvesting techniques but also receive a variety of subsidies from their governments that serve to reduce costs and risks. As subsidies for corn and bean production—the last symbols of Mexico's strictly

symbolic revolutionary commitment to a strong peasant sector—
fall to make way for North American free trade, the ranks of displaced peasants forced into urban underemployment, migratory
labor, or the poverty of genuine subsistence farming will swell by
the millions.

The Salinas administration acknowledged as much in unveil-
ing its Program for the Productive Conversion of the Ministry of
Agriculture in 1992. According to this program, 72 percent of all
corn farmers—representing two million families—are uncompeti-
tive and "will have to search for alternatives in other crops, reor-
ganize their land holdings, . . . associate with private capitalists,
or become wage laborers in rural or urban areas."[35] Mexico's un-
dersecretary for agriculture sees up to thirteen million peasants
forced to abandon the countryside by the year 2010.[36]

Opening agriculture to the international economy has so far
exacerbated Mexico's uneven distribution of wealth and income,
one of the world's most skewed. At the same time, the country has
lost its agricultural trade surplus. Exports are up, but imports
have gone up more. Even if Mexico succeeds in regaining a surplus, however, its economic policies mean that the beneficiaries of
this success will be Mexican and foreign agribusinesses and not
the rural poor. The farmers who have lost their livelihood due to
the failure of government to support small-scale agriculture have
no access to the dollars brought in by export crops.

In some areas of the country the changing agricultural pano-
rama includes a proliferation of foreign-owned facilities, as transnational agribusinesses follow their manufacturing counterparts
by adopting global production, processing, and marketing strategies. Mexico's climate and low-wage work force have made it a
logical location for foreign food packers and processors that seek
to lower the cost of the goods they sell in the United States, Japan,
and Europe.

In Torreón, Coahuila, Tyson Foods employees bone chicken
legs from Arkansas, pack them, and send them to Japan for sale
as frozen yakatori. In Irapuato, Guanajuato, Basic Vegetable Products imports onion seeds, supervises their planting, harvesting,
and processing, and exports dried onion flakes and powder back
to the United States. Amway International has begun to grow ac-
erola cherries in Mexico that will be processed for their vitamin
content in California. Cattle may soon cross the border three

times before reaching consumers, as calves born in Mexico are shipped for feeding to the United States, returned to Mexico for slaughter and packing, and then sent back to the United States for distribution.

Such operations are called agrimaquilas because they import part of their inputs and then export most if not all of their finished food product. These new foreign companies also join a sizable contingent of more traditional foreign agribusinesses already in Mexico. PepsiCo, Ralston Purina, Campbell, Nestlé, Kraft General Foods, Del Monte, Gerber, Kellogg, and other transnationals generally process foods for the domestic market or grow tropical products like bananas, melons, and pineapples for export. Most of these companies came to Mexico in the late 1950s and the 1960s, when Mexican agricultural policy began to encourage foreign investment as a way to modernize the country's food sector.

With globalization catching hold in the food industry, authorized foreign direct investment in Mexican agriculture vaulted from $8.4 million in 1980 to $174 million by the end of 1992.[37] The jump in foreign investment has paralleled—and contributed to— an equally impressive hike in the volume of Mexican exports. Mexican food, beverage, and tobacco exports to the United States have more than doubled since 1980. The United States purchases more than 90 percent of Mexico's agricultural exports, with tomatoes, coffee, and livestock heading the list. And the United States supplies Mexico with roughly 80 percent of its food imports, led by grains—especially corn and sorghum—live animals, meat, and oilseeds. About 20 percent of the coffee consumed in the United States is Mexican, as are 20 percent of the fresh tomatoes and roughly 40 percent of the frozen broccoli.[38]

Despite the presence of dozens of foreign agribusinesses in Mexico, total foreign investment in the agricultural sector represents less than one-half of 1 percent of total authorized foreign direct investment as of December 1992.[39] Nevertheless these firms exert great influence because of their buying power, technology, and marketing skills. In the late 1970s transnational corporations were present in twenty-seven of the forty agricultural subsectors and were responsible for over half of Mexico's production in eleven of them.[40] In crops ranging from oilseeds and sorghum to broccoli and mangoes, transnationals direct seed selection, soil preparation, the timing of the harvest, the marketing of the product, and all steps in between.

Although U.S. corporations form the backbone of Mexico's export-oriented manufacturing and agricultural production, the level of new U.S. investment in productive activities in recent years has fallen below the expectations of the Mexican government. Investment from the United States and other industrial countries has increased but most new investors have been attracted to service sectors such as tourism, which absorbed fully 40 percent of foreign direct investment in 1991, and retailing.

Financial service firms have also flocked to Mexico after Salinas took office, banking on his promised "modernization" campaign to open up the country's financial industry and expecting that Mexico would return to international capital markets for the first time since the 1982 debt crisis. Led by Goldman Sachs, Citibank, and J.P. Morgan, U.S. firms dominated the competition to underwrite Mexico's international bond offerings, which totaled more than $8 billion in 1991. Mergers and acquisitions work proved just as lucrative, driven by joint ventures between foreign and Mexican companies and by the government's privatization drive.[41] Many of these companies hope to open banking operations eventually, as Mexican restrictions on majority-foreign ownership of banks are liberalized either through a free trade agreement or through unilateral changes.

Investment in services is important in stabilizing the country's balance of payments, but it does not have as broad an impact on the economy as manufacturing investment, which generally creates more jobs, produces backward and forward linkages with other economic sectors, and boosts exports. Whereas nearly 80 percent of new direct investment in 1980 was in manufacturing and just 8.5 percent in services, in 1992 almost 60 percent of new foreign direct investment went to service industries and only 27 percent flowed into the manufacturing sector.[42]

To supplement the flow of foreign direct investment and to help tie the larger Mexican companies into international financial markets, President Salinas opened the stock exchange to foreign participation in 1989. In the three years following the opening, more than $7 billion in portfolio or indirect foreign investment entered Mexico—approximately the same amount as new direct foreign investment during the same period.[43] By mid-1992 foreigners, the vast majority from the United States, held nearly 30 percent of the market's total value.

This portfolio investment represents an important source of foreign exchange and demonstrates a new degree of foreign interest and confidence in the Mexican economy. But the buying spree in the Bolsa Mexicana de Valores is not entirely positive, given the volatile character of this type of speculative investment. The ever-present danger is that the dollars that flow into Mexico via the stock market can just as easily and quickly flow out of Mexico. This concern was heightened during the summer of 1992, when foreign investors took billions of dollars out of the market and possibly out of the country.[44] Portfolio investment—unlike direct investment in plant and equipment—makes a weak foundation for national economic stability and development.

The restructuring of the Mexican economy even includes allowing foreigners to play an increasingly important role in petroleum production and processing. Since its nationalization in 1938, the oil industry has symbolized Mexican resistance to Yankee economic imperialism. No Mexican official has yet suggested turning over ownership of oil reserves to foreigners, but regulatory changes are opening up most other aspects of the industry. Since the mid-1980s, the de la Madrid and Salinas administrations reduced from seventy to eight the number of petrochemicals classified as "basic"—and therefore reserved to state-owned operations.[45] The number defined as "secondary"—in which direct foreign ownership is limited to 40 percent—fell from over 700 to sixty-six.[46]

The Salinas administration also split Pemex into four divisions, isolating the ownership and production of petroleum from refining, marketing, and distribution. The reorganization facilitated increased foreign investment in the downstream operations while allowing Mexico to retain ownership over reserves. The changes allowed such transnational corporations as Du Pont, Monsanto, Union Carbide, and Allied Chemical to increase their stakes in the production of petroleum-based chemicals.

But the foreign capital invested in the oil industry by early 1993 fell well short of the $8 billion in outside financing that the Mexican government calculated it needed to maintain export levels and to ensure that domestic energy demands were met. Some Mexican officials have predicted that Mexico will be a net oil importer by the turn of the century if it does not obtain substantial injections of foreign capital for exploration and production. Facing the threat of declining production and reserves, government planners are increasingly recognizing that the traditional goals of using the petroleum industry as a springboard for national development and as a major source of revenue have to be scaled back. If the restructuring of Pemex and the regulatory changes already implemented continue to fail to attract foreign capital, it is likely that all phases of the industry will be opened to foreign participation in the short or medium term, despite the Salinas administration's declarations to the contrary.

The restructuring of Mexico's oil industry and the fact that serious observers are speculating about foreign ownership of oil reserves indicate the extent to which Mexico's relationship with the global economy has changed in less than one decade. Long considered an unreliable partner whose power had to be restricted and channelled by the government, international capital now enjoys virtual carte blanche in Mexico. If this strategy is successful, Mexico has much to gain in the way of expanded access to capital and technology, new jobs, and increased productivity. But given the shocking asymmetry between the two nations, Mexico faces the danger of further restricting its development alternatives by making its trade, labor, and productive core more subject to the condition and direction of the U.S. economy.

Chapter 2

Maquiladoras: Manufacturing on the Margin

Mexico's U-turn from a state-led, inward-looking development path to a neoliberal, export-driven route represented a sudden, dramatic shift in many ways. But one key aspect of the new approach—attracting foreign capital to promote exports and manufacturing employment—had been in place in a restricted form since 1965. In that year the Mexican government opened its northern border to foreign-owned export-processing plants through its Border Industrialization Program. This initiative in effect created an insulated "sub-economy" governed by different rules and subject to different economic forces. On the one hand, the Mexican government encouraged U.S. companies to move to the borderlands and set up maquiladoras, while on the other it discouraged foreign investment in the country's interior with its "Mexicanization" policies.

The Border Industrialization Program was Mexico's first major departure from its strategy of restricting foreign investment and reducing dependence on the international economy. The program waived a number of foreign investment restrictions and import rules for export-oriented assembly plants. With few exceptions, plants set up under this program, called maquiladoras, could be 100 percent foreign-owned.[47] Initially they had to be located within 12.5 miles of the border, but in 1972 the administration of Luís Echeverría eliminated this restriction, prohibiting maquilas only in Mexico's three largest cities: the capital, Guadalajara, and Monterrey.[48]

Originally seen as a gimmick to provide employment to agricultural workers returning after the United States ended the Bracero Program the maquila program had by the mid-1980s become a "priority sector" for Mexico according to President de la Madrid.[49] By the early 1990s export-oriented industrialization and the production-sharing model of the maquilas were central to the Salinas administration's development strategy for Mexico as a whole.

The maquila program works this way: The XYZ Corporation leases land in Tijuana and sets up a wholly owned subsidiary called XYZ de México. XYZ and its U.S. suppliers send leather, electric motors, rubber wheels, and a variety of other parts to the Tijuana maquila. In addition, suppliers in Singapore ship computer chips to the plant. XYZ de México employees assemble the parts into self-propelled golf carts, package them in Mexican-made foam and cardboard, and send them to an XYZ Corporation warehouse in Chula Vista, where they are stamped "Made in America." XYZ de México pays no Mexican duties on any of the imported parts, and XYZ Corporation pays U.S. duties only on the value of the Singaporean computer chips, the Mexican packaging, and the value of the Mexican labor.[50]

The Border Industrialization Program represented the first step toward the integration of Mexico into the U.S. manufacturing base. But regional integration was hardly what Mexico had in mind in establishing the program. Until the mid-1980s the country's economic planners viewed it largely as an employment program. Although employee training is an additional potential benefit, most jobs are unskilled and many positions in engineering and management (with the exception of personnel administration) are held by foreigners.

Along with allowing full foreign ownership, the most attractive aspect of the Border Industrialization Program for foreign manufacturers is the exemption from duties of all imported inputs—materials, components, machinery, and tools. To qualify for these exemptions, a firm is required to ship all waste and scrap by-products out of the country along with the finished product and to post a bond for the value of the duties that were waived. This latter requirement led to the phrase "in-bond assembly operations," which is used interchangeably with maquiladoras and maquilas.

By any name the program has changed the face of Mexico's northern border region. Industrial parks have sprouted up from Tijuana to Matamoros, and around them maquila workers and other impoverished border residents have constructed shantytowns. Maquila operations span a very wide range of activities, from the assembly of plastic toys and polyester lingerie to the highly complex management of a modern lumber mill. At eight maquiladoras owned by the A.C. Nielsen company, workers sort millions of coupons for U.S. manufacturers and retailers. Catalina

Offshore Products sends U.S. sea urchins to its maquiladora in Ensenada for processing into sushi. At the Allen Coach Works plant in Nuevo Laredo, workers saw Cadillacs and Lincoln Continentals in half and then refashion the luxury cars into limousines. Despite the shift from a regional to a national development program, the maquila sector remains concentrated on the northern border. It is here where foreign investors find the combination of cheap labor, proximity to U.S. markets and suppliers, and infrastructure that best enhances their competitive advantage. About 80 percent of the assembly plants are still found along Mexico's northern border, mostly in the major cities of Juárez, Tijuana, Nogales, Mexicali, Matamoros, Reynosa, and Nuevo Laredo.[51] In search of still cheaper labor, some firms have established plants as far away from the border as the Yucatán and Oaxaca, while others looking for an untapped skilled labor market have set up maquilas in such places as Guadalajara, Chihuahua and Hermosillo. But proximity to U.S. suppliers and the U.S. market ensures that the border will the premier location for export-processing industries, even after a U.S.-Mexico free trade accord.

From Screwdrivers to Robots

Maquila trade—imported inputs to Mexico and exported assembled goods to the United States—constitutes one-third of the two-way trade between the two nations. Economic changes and aggressive promotion have prompted rapid growth in the maquiladora program. The number of assembly plants jumped from 585 in 1982 to 1,125 in 1987, and 2,160 by mid-1993. The number of employees grew even faster, due to the increasing size of the average plant's work force.

Not only have the numbers of factories and workers increased since the 1960s, the types of industries setting up maquiladoras have also dramatically changed. No longer do low-tech or so-called "screwdriver" industries dominate the maquila sector. Instead, electronics and auto-parts plants that increasingly feature high-tech production systems are the leading industries—together accounting for about half the maquila work force and value-added production. Automatic insertion machines and surface-mount technology have been added to circuit board assembly lines, clean rooms to the semiconductor industry, and robots to metal-machining processes. Value added per employee—one indication of the technological level of a process—increased from $5,780 in 1983 to $7,794 in 1989.[52] As Ford's engine plant in Chihuahua and dozens of other state-of-the-art Mexican facilities demonstrate, Mexican workers are quite capable of turning out high-quality, high-technology products.

Border towns such as Juárez and Mexicali have become high-tech centers for leading defense and aeronautical corporations such as Hughes Aircraft, TRW, Rockwell, McDonnell-Douglas, and Bell and Howell. Auditors and quality-control agents from the Defense Contract Administration Services regularly cross the border to monitor the military-related manufacturing in the maquila plants.

Jobs, Jobs, Jobs

On a certain level the success of the Border Industrialization Program is beyond dispute. The economic boom of Mexico's northern cities is largely attributable to the maquiladoras, and the U.S. border cities have benefited from an associated service industry and a healthy commercial sector fueled by the maquila boom and population growth. Although it is not hard to find critics of the pay levels and the environmental repercussions of the maquila industry, most border residents support the presence of the maquila industry. Especially in Mexico, they recognize it as a major source of jobs.

As an employment-generating strategy, the Border Industrialization Program has certainly worked. Unemployment in most Mexican border cities is lower than elsewhere in Mexico. From around 20,000 employees in 1970 maquila employment grew to nearly 130,000 in 1980 and to over 500,000 by the end of 1992 (see Table 1). A recent survey in Nogales, Sonora, found that 45 percent of the work force in that Mexican city was directly or indirectly tied to the maquila industry.[53]

Mexico's net income from the program—the vast majority of which corresponds to workers' wages—replaced tourism as the country's second largest source of foreign exchange in the late 1980s. In 1992 nearly $5 billion flowed to Mexico's central bank as maquila owners traded dollars for pesos to pay their workers and other costs in Mexico.[54] Only oil exports, worth almost $8 billion in 1992, earned more foreign currency. Direct investment in maquiladora plants and equipment brings in another few hundred million dollars in an average year.[55] The low wage rates caused by the devaluation of the Mexican peso sparked the maquila boom of the 1980s. These wages—lower

Table 1. Maquila Industry by Plants, Employees, Value Added, and Labor Cost, 1967-1992

Year	Number of Plants	Employees	Value Added[a]	Avg. Hourly Labor Cost in Maquilas[b]
1967	72	4,000	77	
1968	112	10,927	81	
1969	149	15,900	81	
1970	160	20,327	86	
1971	205	28,483	102	
1972	339	48,060	152	
1973	400	64,330	201	
1974	455	75,977	218	
1975	454	67,214	321	
1976	448	74,496	352	
1977	443	78,433	315	
1978	457	90,704	439	
1979	540	111,365	638	
1980	620	119,546	771	$2.41
1981	605	130,973	974	2.57
1982	585	127,048	812	1.78
1983	600	150,867	825	1.28
1984	672	199,684	1,161	1.43
1985	760	211,968	1,266	1.39
1986	890	249,833	1,295	1.02
1987	1125	305,523	1,635	1.04
1988	1396	369,489	2,339	1.17
1989	1655	429,725	3,057	1.30
1990[c]	1930	460,293	3,362	1.34
1991[d]	1954	489,000	4,100	1.60
1992[e]	2129	511,000	4,300	1.64

a. In millions of current (not adjusted) dollars.
b. Includes direct wages and all benefits, including bonuses, payroll taxes, and vacations. Figures are in 1992 dollars, based on current dollar figures from the Bureau of the Census (unpublished data) and the national CPI in the United States.
c. Data from INEGI cited in *SourceMex* (Latin America Data Base: Albuquerque, NM).
d. Estimates for 1991 provided by Asesoría Económica Especializada (Mexico, D.F.), cited by *SourceMex* (Latin America Data Base, Albuquerque, NM).
e. INEGI data cited by *SourceMex* (Latin America Data Base, Albuquerque, NM, August 25, 1993).

SOURCES: Data for 1967 to 1974 are from Leslie Sklair, *Assembling for Development: The Maquila Industry in Mexico and the United States* (Winchester, MA: Unwin Hyman, 1989), 54; data from 1975 to 1989 are from Instituto Nacional de Estadística, Geografía, e Informática (INEGI), *Estadística de la Industria Maquiladora de Exportación* (Mexico, D.F., various years).

than those paid in other leading export-processing centers and lower than those paid by Mexican manufacturers—are not nearly enough to provide for a family, and they keep many maquila workers living in makeshift homes in squatter colonies that often lack water and sewerage.[56] Even as the maquiladoras incorporate sophisticated technology and higher value-added activities into their assembly systems, wages remain extremely low: about $60 per forty-five-hour week on average, including benefits.[57] In fact, if wages and benefits had kept pace with advancing productivity through the 1980s, average Mexican compensation would have been almost 80 percent higher in 1990, according to one study.[58]

Instead of attempting to reduce high turnover rates and to increase worker productivity by offering higher wages, maquiladora managers entice workers with such perks as free lunches, beauty contests, company transportation, showers at work, and company-sponsored sports. Rather than raise wages, advised an article in *Twin Plant News*, "there are some things you can do to help, such as setting up a clothing exchange in the plant. . . . Buy some bulk food items such as flour, beans, potatoes, etc., and distribute these among your employees."[59]

Maquila associations in every important city share information about their members' wage structure. The wage reports serve as guidelines and help ensure that companies do not enter a bidding war for the available labor force. Although the associations deny that their intention is to hold down wages, numerous investigators have found that maquila managers feel great pressure from their peers to maintain wages within a certain range.[60] The government aids employers in this endeavor, according to managers of two U.S.-owned auto plants. "We even get help from the government making sure that we don't settle too high" in negotiations with the union, said one. "The labor ministry takes an active part in negotiations, especially in companies our size. And they steer the level of increases," confirmed another.[61]

Extremely low wages produce high employee turnover in the maquiladoras as workers jump at any opportunity to earn more money. It is common for plants to lose one-tenth of their entire work forces in some months and to see more employees quit in one year than are employed at any given time.

Although some employers complain that such turnover costs them a significant amount of money because of the constant need to retrain new workers, for most maquiladoras turnover is at worst a minor annoyance and sometimes even helpful. Only a handful of maquiladoras provide more than a day or two of training for their assembly-line positions—where pay is lowest and turnover highest—and for many training lasts only a few hours.[62] In those plants that do provide greater training, it is generally provided only to workers with a minimum level of seniority—usually at least three months. Since most turnover occurs before this cutoff point, few workers with significant amounts of training actually leave their jobs.

Many maquiladoras produce consumer goods marked by highly variable demand in the United States. The size of the work force in these plants can drop by more than one-fourth from December to January. In these cases high turnover relieves management of the need to meet legal requirements for laying off workers.[63]

Managers are clearly aware that raising wages would reduce turnover, yet the problem is not grave enough to have provoked wage hikes. According to a manager at one plant with 100 percent turnover in 1990, workers quit because "the pay is poor, the work is heavy, and the company always asks for more."[64] High turnover rates create a false feeling that unemployment is low along the border. Official statistics indicate that unemployment hovers around 3 percent in border towns. This figure is meaningless, however, since the government counts as employed anyone who worked at least one hour during the previous week, including through "self-employment" like washing the windows of cars stopped at street lights. The fact is that earnings in the informal sector often surpass those paid by maquiladoras, leading many to opt for underemployment.[65]

Enclave Industrialization

Much as it had during the *porfiriato*, foreign investment in the maquiladoras has created an enclave economy. It is an economy geographically located within Mexico but largely dependent on decisions made by corporate executives, consumers, and policy makers in the United States, and it generates few benefits for that part of society outside the enclave.

A major failure of the Border Industrialization program has been its inability to spur the creation of linkages with the rest of the Mexican economy. This means that few Mexican industries, either along the border or elsewhere in Mexico, supply the maquiladoras. Neither do many Mexican businesses buy maquila-manufactured goods that are then used as part of their own production process. Consequently, the beneficial impact in northern Mexico of the maquila sector is largely limited to job creation and the economic activity generated by worker spending.[66]

The logic of the maquiladora program, which relies on minimal government interference in corporate decisions to encourage foreign investment, has stifled efforts to extend its benefits beyond the creation of jobs. Mexican attempts to build linkages between the maquiladoras and the rest of the economy—through supply contracts or technology transfer, for example—have failed. Throughout the program the proportion of the value of production in maquiladoras that comes from Mexican-owned businesses has been under 2 percent.[67]

Because of its lack of linkages with the domestic economy and its export orientation, the maquila industry can be fairly described as a foreign-owned enclave economy. But the maquilas do not operate independently of the government and local capitalists. From the beginning of the Border Industrialization Program, a close partnership has developed among the Mexican state bureaucracy, the domestic economic elite, and the transnational corporations that operate the maquilas.[68] Not only has the government financed construction of numerous industrial parks, but it has also supported the maquilas by providing land, roads, and public utilities—and by leaving them virtually untaxed and unregulated.

By keeping a tight lid on independent union activity and by having government-affiliated labor confederations work closely with the maquila management, the Mexican government has also sided with the interests of the maquila sector to the detriment of Mexican workers.[69] In the mid-1970s, when labor organizing was threatening to drive wages up, the government and the maquila industry even entered into an "Alliance for Production."[70] Shortly thereafter the Confederation of Mexican Workers (CTM), the official labor confederation, regained control of the plants, independent organizing was suppressed, and the peso was devalued, all of which made Mexico once again a desirable offshore location for production-sharing industries. So compatible are the industry and official unions that many corporations actually favor having a union to reduce the turnover rate and increase productivity.[71]

Like the government, Mexican capitalists and professionals play an important role in making the maquila sector work smoothly. Their most important role is facilitating maquila operations by managing industrial parks, providing legal and accounting services, arranging transportation, and serving as customs brokers.[72] In each of the main border cities, a local bourgeoisie feeds off of the maquila sector.[73] According to one estimate, the Mexican companies that run the industrial parks can clear as much as fifty cents an hour per maquila employee.[74] The most powerful of these maquila service firms is Grupo Bermúdez of Juárez, founded by Antonio Bermúdez, the same man who had run the government's nationalist PRONAF (National Border Program) campaign in the early 1960s.[75]

Whereas the Mexican government has gone to great lengths to assist the maquila industry and shelter it from labor and environmental regulations, it has largely ignored the basic needs of the maquila work force. And maquila-based development has accentuated the planning and infrastructural problems faced by Mexican cities. Most obvious are the housing crisis and the lack of waste disposal and wastewater treatment facilities. Electricity, water, and roads were extended to the maquiladoras, but little thought was given to the social and environmental costs of the maquila boom. The small amount of revenue collected from the maquiladoras goes not to local governments but to the national treasury, leaving Mexican border towns no funds to cope with immense public health and housing problems. So grave are some of these problems that Juárez at one point even began to discourage new maquila growth.

At a time when growing environmental consciousness, high labor turnover, and urban congestion are making the border region less desirable, some companies are finding advantages in establishing maquiladoras deeper in Mexico. New communications and transportation networks will make nonborder locations increasingly attractive, especially considering the still lower labor costs of most nonborder sites.

When the Border Industrialization Program became a centerpiece of Mexico's new export-oriented development strategy in the 1980s, policy makers had in mind the relative success of Taiwan and South Korea. But unlike these Asian tigers, Mexico has failed to use the maquila sector as a stepping-stone to full-fledged industrialization.[76]

Recent trade and investment liberalization initiatives on the part of the Mexican government show no sign of sparking more integral development. Thus far there is nothing to indicate that Mexico will be able to foster more meaningful technology transfer or increase the economic linkages outside the foreign-owned enclave.[77] In the absence of local-content regulations and an active government role in linking suppliers with exporters, companies have little incentive to seek out local firms and work with them to improve quality and reliability.

The most fervent proponents of export-processing industrialization assert that Mexico is poised for an economic takeoff. But a visit to any one of the maquila zones that hug the border gives one a more sobering picture of Mexico's prospects for converting maquila production into broader economic development. Hundreds of workers in Nogales, Sonora, produce automatic garage door openers for Sears at a massive warehouse-style factory, and many live in hovels of their own making just outside the high barbed-wire fence surrounding the plant. Like many other maquila workers, their homes are worth less than the products they assemble every day. Can economic growth and prosperity be the product of such misery?

No matter how many maquilas come to Mexico, it is unlikely that development will follow unless the government aggressively promotes more linkages with domestic producers, genuine technology transfer, and better wages and conditions for the maquila work force. In addition, economic growth will actually subvert development unless it is environmentally sustainable and its costs and benefits are fairly distributed.

The problems of environmental destruction, inadequate social infrastructure, and the exploitation of the country's work force are not attributable solely to the maquilas or the government's export-oriented development strategy. Rather, they are symptoms of Mexico's failure to shape economic policies that ensure that the benefits of economic development are broadly shared. However, ensuring that investment and technology nurture broad-based and sustained development will require the Mexican government to assume more control over the nature and direction of export-oriented manufacturing—an increasingly difficult task as economic globalization proceeds along neoliberal lines.

The danger, as industry spokespeople are fond of repeating, is that government regulation, such as increased minimum wages or mandatory local-supply requirements, will kill the goose that lays the golden eggs. This is the same implied threat, of course, that industries are using against the U.S. government and U.S. workers. Although few people outside of the maquila business sector would describe the eggs laid by the maquilas as golden, a future without these assembly plants looks even grimmer than the present economic reality.

As many maquila workers are well aware, their wages are low—but not as low as those being paid in places such as Haiti and Malaysia or, for that matter, by the maquila sector farther south in their own country. Although companies publicly talk of relocating to lower-wage locations mainly as an idle threat to keep wages low and the government cooperative, some maquilas have indeed closed down and moved to Southeast Asia.[78] Increasingly, the structure and the mobility of global production limit the development choices open to Mexico and its borderlands.

The Runaway Phenomenon

The flip side of the enclave nature of the maquiladoras within Mexico is their function viewed from the United States as an appendage of the U.S. economy. The finished products and the profits from the operation generally go to the United States, but the production is exempt from U.S. laws and enforcement. In effect, a corporation with maquila production is importing Mexican labor to the United States but employing the workers according to Mexican laws.[79] The Mexican government recognizes this aspect of the maquila production process. Mexican trade statistics ignore the in-bond import of components for assembly and the export of the finished products or subassemblies. Instead the government's trade department counts the value of wages paid to maquiladora employees as an export of a service—called the service of transformation—to the United States.[80]

Whether this is a service the United States should import is the central question in a debate that has raged since the mid-1960s. A primary focus of the debate is the Offshore Assembly

Provision of U.S. tariff law. Existing in various forms since 1930, this provision allows firms to import goods without paying duties on any U.S.-made components or materials that were used to produce those goods.[81] The provision thus makes it cheaper for U.S.-based manufacturers to take advantage of in-bond programs like Mexico's Border Industrialization Program. Proponents of the tariff exemption argue that it preserves U.S. jobs by encouraging manufacturers to use U.S.-made components and materials in their foreign assembly operations. Opponents argue that it destroys U.S. jobs by encouraging manufacturers to set up foreign assembly operations in the first place.

The American Federation of Labor and Congress of Industrial Organizations (AFL-CIO) used this latter argument in 1967, when it first went on record opposing these tariff breaks.[82] At that time Mexico was but one host country among many, and the U.S. industrial base did not seem nearly as weak as it now is. Hundreds of corporations sent their labor-intensive and easily transportable work to duty-free "export-processing zones" in east Asia or the Caribbean. Although transportation costs to those locations were often higher than they were to Mexico, political and regulatory factors—including a receptive attitude toward foreign investors and control over organized labor—often were more important in siting decisions.

In 1968, 112 Mexican maquiladoras assembled or processed approximately $40 million worth of U.S. inputs for duty-free reexport to the United States.[83] This represented less than 15 percent of the total value of goods the United States imported duty-free under the Offshore Assembly Provision that year.[84] By 1977 Mexico had eaten into the market share of export-processing zones in east Asia and the Caribbean. That year the duty-free portion of maquila exports to the United States totaled $631.1 million—32 percent of the global total (see Table 2). Another nine years later, in 1986, the number of maquiladoras had climbed to 890 and the value of U.S. components they imported, processed, and exported had more than quintupled to $3.4 billion. Since that year Mexico has processed more U.S. inputs for duty-free export to the United States than all other countries combined, which continues to be the case today.

Given the large and growing volume of goods entering the United States duty-free under the Offshore Assembly Provision, it is not surprising that the OAP is controversial. From 1968 through the 1980s the AFL-CIO tried numerous times to scuttle the provision: twice in 1969, once each in 1971 and 1974, with twenty-two separate bills in 1976, and on four occasions in the early and mid-1980s. But viewed in isolation, the effects of the OAP are not great.[85] On the one hand, the provision adds somewhat to the demand for U.S. inputs by creating what is in effect a 5 to 10 percent price advantage over equivalent foreign materials. These inputs help support manufacturing jobs in the United States. On the other hand, the provision increases U.S. demand for products assembled abroad. This is because in most industries the tariff exemption lowers the cost of imported products that use duty-free U.S. components. If there were no exemption, domestic assemblers using domestic components would have a small cost advantage over assemblers located abroad. In this way the OAP tends to decrease U.S. employment.

When seen in the light of the broader debate over economic strategy, the OAP—and the U.S. economy's relationship to maquiladoras in general—takes on much greater significance. The arguments against encouraging U.S. investment in the maquiladoras are often the same ones heard in opposition to NAFTA. Indeed, the open trade and investment rules characterizing the maquila program and the OAP have provided a preview of the most controver-

Table 2. *Imports under the Offshore Assembly Provision*[a]
(in millions of U.S. dollars)

	1975	1983	1991
Total OAP imports from all sources	5,162.4	21,575.9	57,527
OAP imports from Mexico	1,019.8	3,714.9	14,335.8
Duty-free portion of imports from all sources	1,265.9	5,386.6	14,517.2
Duty-free portion of imports from Mexico	552.4	1,968.7	7,254.9

a. Known as TSUS 806.30 and 807.00 until 1990 and as HTS 9802.00.60 and 9802.00.80 from 1990 to the present.

SOURCE: Official statistics of the U.S. Department of Commerce, Bureau of the Census.

sial part of NAFTA: the ability of U.S. companies to relocate operations to Mexico and export their products and services back to the U.S. market unimpeded. Hundreds of manufacturers and service providers have done just that since the 1960s, leaving behind hundreds of thousands of U.S. workers and their communities.[86]

This movement is known as the runaway plant phenomenon. Although companies have "run away" to a multitude of low-wage export-processing zones across the globe, nowhere is the phenomenon more visible than right across the border in Mexico. One of the first companies to shift work to Mexico was Fairchild Electronics, which opened a maquiladora in Tijuana in 1966 to take over component assembly previously performed in California. Sears, Roebuck and Co. gave a boost to the program by pushing its suppliers to shift some or all of their work to Mexico. Sears wanted to trim suppliers' costs but keep the "Made in America" label on its products.[87] Dozens of apparel and appliance manufacturers took the huge retailer's advice. Other Fortune 500 companies followed slowly but surely, along with hundreds of smaller firms, many of which went belly-up after a few years of operation.

By no means were all new maquiladoras runaways. In a few cases, old product lines using proven technology were sent to Mexico, to be replaced in this country by newer, top-of-the-line goods. In some others, maquiladoras replaced facilities elsewhere—usually in east Asia. But in hundreds of cases the new Mexican assembly plants were tied to corporate decisions to replace higher-wage U.S. production, either directly or through contract bidding in which low-cost maquiladoras won out over their U.S. competitors.

Near the beginning of the maquiladora program Mexico was sensitive to the charge that it was stealing jobs from U.S. workers. In 1968 the Mexican government claimed that no existing maquiladoras were runaways and pledged to reject any firm that planned to lay off U.S. workers as part of its move to Mexico.[88] Mexico backed off somewhat from this patently absurd claim in 1970. But it continued to maintain that the maquiladoras were not significantly harming U.S. workers and that the government was "carefully reviewing applications" to ensure that no runaways set up shop in the country.[89]

There is no evidence that Mexico believed its own claims. The Ministry of Commerce and Industrial Development was not even able to keep track of those maquiladoras operating in the country at any one time. In any case the pretense was later dropped, when it became apparent that labor's allies in the U.S. Congress were unable to cancel the Offshore Assembly Provision. Increasingly, entrepreneurs were promoting the maquiladora concept to healthy corporations as well as to those suffering from low-cost competitive challenges. By the mid-1970s U.S. giants such as Zenith, General Motors, General Electric, Westinghouse, Parker-Hannifin, Du Pont, ITT, Quaker Oats, Honeywell, Burroughs, and Motorola had joined RCA and Fairchild in establishing maquiladoras.

The U.S. tariff exemption for offshore assembly of U.S. components encouraged the growing exodus of manufacturing to Mexico, and it is likely that Mexico's weak and laxly enforced environmental and labor standards also played a role.[90] But by far the most important factor in the choice of Mexico as an export-processing site was—and is—the low wages paid to Mexican workers. This was made clear by the rapid expansion of maquiladoras after Mexico's minimum wage fell from a high of $1.53 per hour in 1982 to $.68 per hour in 1983, and then to a range around $.50 per hour from 1986 through 1990.[91] Whereas in 1981 Mexican workers were paid more in dollar terms than were workers in South Korea, Taiwan, Hong Kong, and Singapore, by 1983 their wage and benefits package had moved into last place among the five countries.[92]

Armed with wage figures such as these and with increasing evidence of high-quality production in Mexico, maquiladora promoters found their jobs easier and easier. In brochures, videos, seminars, and personal visits, companies like Assemble in Mexico, Cal Pacifico, IMEC, and Inter-American Holdings claimed they could save the right kind of firm between $10,000 and $22,000 per year for each job transferred to Mexico. The U.S. government even got into the act. In 1986 the Department of Commerce co-sponsored Expo-Maquila '86, a business conference held in Acapulco at which investors were told of the savings they could enjoy by moving some or all of their production from the United States to Mexico. When the U.S. Congress found out that taxpayer money was being used to encourage runaway plants, it required that the practice be halted, but of course the expositions have continued without U.S. government assistance.[93] During the Salinas administration the Mexican government helped establish two development funds, called Amerimex and Ventana, to assist Mexicans who want either to purchase U.S.-based companies and move them to Mexico, or to form a joint venture with a U.S. firm for that purpose.

Runaway plants added to the epidemic of plant closings that wreaked havoc in cities and towns across the United States during the 1980s. A network of community- and labor-based activists formed in response to this epidemic. These activists usually focused on immediate issues such as dissuading local companies from shutting down and pushing for a national requirement that companies give their workers advance notice of plans to close down a facility.

Toward the end of the decade the movement to halt plant closings focused increasingly on the issue of manufacturing relocation to low-wage areas around the world and especially to Mexico. In doing so these activists hooked up with a second grassroots network largely made up of church-based groups and progressive political organizations. Concerned with issues of corporate responsibility, this group of activists had enjoyed comparative success in drawing attention to U.S. corporate support for the apartheid South African regime and in attaching a stigma to foreign investment in that country.

Hoping to accomplish similar objectives in Mexico, the two networks joined forces with national labor unions, the AFL-CIO, and two grassroots Mexican organizations. In early 1991 they announced the formation of the Coalition for Justice in the Maquiladoras. The coalition vowed to push for minimum standards of corporate behavior in Mexico's maquiladora industry, including observance of U.S. environmental and occupational health standards, and fair employment practices.[94] The coalition's guiding principle—that corporations should act just as responsibly in poor countries as they are expected to in wealthy ones—became a centerpiece of later efforts to establish minimum environmental and labor standards as part of any North American free trade agreement.

Whither the Maquiladoras under Free Trade?

Talk of free trade raised questions about the future of the maquila sector. At the very least Mexico would have to revamp the legal framework of the Border Industrialization Program. Since the ability to import parts duty-free into Mexico from the United States would no longer remain unique to maquiladoras, there would be no need for in-bond treatment of those imports. In addition, requiring certain manufacturers to export their production would become meaningless when those exports could re-enter Mexico duty-free.[95]

The NAFTA text signed in late 1992 required Mexico to phase out the maquiladora program over the course of seven years. But few, if any, of the maquiladoras themselves would be forced out of business by the pact. Many maquila managers had feared that their reliance on Asian components would disqualify their products for duty-free status under NAFTA. The amounts in question are not small. Roughly 45 percent of all maquila inputs have traditionally originated outside the United States and Mexico. In the end, though, negotiators adopted a loose rule of origin, as it is called, for most industries. To qualify for duty-free status a product that came into North America under one tariff heading had only to be transformed sufficiently within the continent to be classified under a different tariff heading. Even if no tariff classification change occurred, up to 40 percent of the value of a product was allowed to originate outside the North American region without invalidating that product's duty-free status. These rules posed little threat to most maquiladoras.

Of greater importance to maquila operators were the special restrictions tacked on to a number of the sector's most prominent products—auto parts, televisions, computers, and textiles. As a result of strong lobbying efforts by politically powerful U.S. industries, producers of these goods will either have to meet higher regional content requirements or incorporate specific regionally produced components to gain duty-free status.[96]

Although these special restrictions demonstrate that NAFTA—like all regional free trade agreements—is as much about managing trade as freeing it, they are unlikely to cause many maquiladoras to close up shop. Most producers that do not currently meet the regional-content rules will be able to shift sources of supply relatively quickly. After analyzing NAFTA's provisions, one major economic-forecasting firm predicted the maquiladora industry would grow by an average annual rate of 8.5 percent from 1993 to 1997.[97]

Chapter 3

Labor Solidarity Faces the Test

As the experience of Mexico's maquiladoras demonstrates, what ties workers in different countries together is not an abstract concept of worker solidarity but the concrete phenomenon of economic globalization. The internationalization of capital has put workers on the defensive as they seek to defend their rights, their wages, and their jobs, but there is a silver lining. Labor organizations are beginning to respond to globalization by stepping up efforts to forge international alliances and to question the long-term effectiveness of existing strategies.

This does not mean that the internationalization of capital will achieve the goal that eluded Karl Marx and Friedrich Engels— uniting the world's workers. Nationalism and immediate self-interest still pose huge barriers. But it is increasingly clear both to union officials and rank-and-file members that the internationalization of organized labor, in a variety of forms, has to be part of the solution. Although practical movement in this direction is still very limited, nowhere is the trend toward greater cross-border work more evident than in North America. A new international outlook for U.S. labor would of course have to extend beyond this hemisphere.[98] But North America is the first testing ground, and whether optimism or pessimism is warranted will be determined by the evolution of nascent U.S.-Mexico-Canada labor ties.

The maquiladora boom, partly fueled by runaway plants, made Mexico one of the most important countries for U.S. unions to develop a practical approach to international labor solidarity. But neither the AFL-CIO nor the major industrial unions made an effort to reach out to Mexican unions as partners until the early 1990s. For the most part organized labor failed to recognize the growing interdependence of the United States and Mexico, or failed to respond to the process. As a result, cross-border work remained limited to isolated efforts by relatively small unions (or by a few individuals within larger unions) until recently.

Farm labor unions, many of whose members are Mexican immigrants, led the way in transboundary work with Mexican organizations. Beginning in 1979 the Arizona Farm Workers union won clauses in many of its labor contracts requiring employers to contribute ten (and later twenty) cents per worker-hour to a development fund. The fund paid for agricultural and community projects in the workers' hometowns in Mexico.

In 1987 the Ohio-based Farm Labor Organizing Committee (FLOC) sought help from the National Union of Farm Workers (SNTOAC) in Mexico. A year earlier, during FLOC's negotiations with Campbell Soup, the company threatened to move tomato paste production to Mexico, where it already operated a cannery. Backed by a national boycott of Campbell's products, FLOC overcame this threat and won a unique three-way agreement between the union, Campbell, and family farmers who grew under contract with Campbell.

Anticipating Campbell's use of Mexico as a bargaining tool in future negotiations, FLOC leader Baldemar Velasquez asked the AFL-CIO to arrange a meeting with Fidel Velázquez of the Confederation of Mexican Workers (CTM). The CTM chief in turn introduced Velasquez to SNTOAC leader Diego Aguilar, who represents workers at Campbell's tomato paste factory in Sinaloa. The two unions reached an agreement, and Velasquez returned to Mexico the next year to watch the harvest and visit Campbell's operations.

FLOC and SNTOAC launched the U.S.-Mexico Exchange Program at that time, and they have continued to exchange information and develop bargaining strategies to work for "wage vs. living cost parity," full employment, protection of "guest workers" in the United States, and the development of "strong and democratic" unions in both countries. In 1989 FLOC's solidarity and the mobilization of its support network helped SNTOAC win a wage increase some 15 percent higher than the government's legal cap for that year. In FLOC's own negotiations with Campbell that same year, "not once did we hear any mention of Mexico," according to Velasquez.

Until 1990 none of the industrial unions came close to forging similarly close ties with Mexican counterparts. This failure occurred despite the fact that U.S. corporations frequently threatened to ship work to Mexico during contract negotiations, and despite the ties that the AFL-CIO has maintained with the CTM, the principal Mexican labor organization.

The AFL-CIO provides training in the United States for up to twenty CTM staff members each year in a program funded by the U.S. Agency for International Development, and until recently it posted a full-time staff person to CTM headquarters in Mexico City. But the U.S. labor federation has been unable to parlay its relationship with the CTM into an effective organizing drive among export-oriented assembly plants, the part of the Mexican economy of greatest importance to U.S. workers. CTM officials have repeatedly promised to make organizing these plants—especially the maquiladoras—a priority, and just as repeatedly have committed themselves to encouraging the growth of the industry by ensuring labor peace. In 1966, the year Mexico's Border Industrialization Program took effect, CTM leader Fidel Velázquez pledged that "the CTM would not pressure without cause the industrialists who come to [the border] . . . On the contrary, in every occasion, it would support those investments, avoiding unjustified labor-management conflicts."[99]

Velázquez and most of his regional deputies appear to have upheld this pledge. In the mid-1970s the official unions collaborated with the government and maquila employers to crush a series of strikes and the independent labor groups that organized them. In 1983 Velázquez himself intervened to break a strike at Zenith's Reynosa plant—then the largest maquiladora in the country—twice nullifying elections for local CTM officials and cooperating with Zenith's forced resignation of ten local activists.[100] In 1989, after the CTM won an interunion battle for representation at a number of plants in Reynosa, Velázquez reportedly promised visiting members of the U.S. Congress that there would be no further labor problems.[101]

There is not necessarily a contradiction between Velázquez' commitments to organize the maquiladoras and to promote the industry. The maquiladora program competes directly with low-wage export-processing zones around the globe, and one of the principal arenas of competition is the stability of the work force. Attracting investors means controlling worker activism, and the most direct way the CTM and other official unions can do that is to organize workers under their own banners. Accounts abound of the efficiency with which official unions perform this function.

The Jalisco Maquila Association, for example, has advised new members to accept the CTM, "especially since unions in Guadalajara tend to facilitate rather than impede internal plant relations."

The founder of Mexico's first industrial park, located in Ciudad Juárez, had nothing but praise for the city's labor chief in 1981: "Luis Vidal has always been understanding. He has been a big help to us, and I think it's been to our advantage to have a labor leader like Vidal—very, very advantageous."[102] The general manager of an assembly plant in Reynosa was even more explicit: "We had some labor problems, so along with a dozen other plants we went to Mexico City to make a special arrangement with the CTM. It was time-consuming and expensive, but we arranged to have a special union leader that our companies can deal with . . . . If you have any disruptions in the plant, they are very helpful with that, too."[103]

The CTM's reluctance to stray from government economic policy and its repression of independent labor activists who might take a more militant stand have not persuaded the AFL-CIO to support other unions or independent organizing efforts. Until recently, the federation failed even to expand its contacts outside of official union circles. The reason most frequently cited for this commitment to the CTM is the weakness of the independent union movements—it makes more sense, in this view, to work with an imperfect partner that can get something done than with a partner that agrees on all the issues but is powerless.

But the AFL-CIO's history abroad suggests that another reason for its past failure to support democratic union movements in Mexico may be the U.S. federation's interest in political stability, which includes preventing the emergence of leftist labor movements.[104] Yet another likely reason is that established unions and labor federations in all countries are reluctant to deal with dissident movements abroad for fear of setting a precedent. As one academic observer of international labor relations noted, many union leaders believe that "as soon as you start dealing with nonofficial labor unions in other countries, you open it up to their dealing with nonofficial bodies in this country."[105]

Like the federation itself, most AFL-CIO affiliates either worked with the CTM or had little involvement with Mexican unions until the late 1980s. In some cases, U.S. union leaders even rejected the approaches of independent Mexican labor groups. The September 19th National Garment Workers Union—named for the date of Mexico City's devastating 1985 earthquake—provides a case in point. Seeking international support for its fledgling organizing effort among the seamstresses of Mexico City's sweatshops, September 19th union representatives traveled to New York and then across the country to Los Angeles, visiting the headquarters and a number of locals of the two largest U.S. garment workers' unions. The Mexicans were largely ignored by the hierarchy of the International Ladies Garment Workers Union and the Amalgamated Clothing and Textile Workers Union (ACTWU). What is more, both headquarters sent instructions to their locals "warning them not to receive the visitors, since they weren't part of the CTM," according to a U.S. labor activist working with the visiting group. This attitude was especially surprising in the case of ACTWU, since the union was an outspoken opponent of the AFL-CIO's policies in Central America at the time.

"The [U.S.] unions were uninterested" in the visit, according to a former ACTWU staff member. "Mexico just didn't exist in the minds of the trade union hierarchy at the time. All they talked about was the Caribbean Basin Initiative."[106] But the farther the Mexican workers got from New York, the more receptive U.S. unionists were. In Los Angeles, local leaders organized a Labor Solidarity Network to support the new union's efforts. They were forced to do so informally, however, without official union backing.

NAFTA Sounds a Wake-up Call

When NAFTA came off the drawing boards in the early 1990s the U.S. labor movement was in crisis, having been weakened and demoralized by plant closures, import competition, and extreme political hostility during the previous decade. Efforts to reverse the declining position of U.S. workers were mostly unsuccessful. The labor movement's "Buy American" strategy of voluntary and legislated protectionism, for example, alienated large segments of the general public while failing to produce long-term solutions.[107] And the strategy of wage concessions and cooperative labor relations adopted by many unions during the 1980s collided with the $1.50/hour reality of low-wage competition under NAFTA, raising the question of just how low workers would have to go to retain their jobs.

In addition to tactics like protectionism and concession bargaining, U.S. labor tried to shore up its position by seeking legislation to reduce plant closings, protect specific industries, fund
worker retraining, and condition access to the U.S. market on
respect for international labor rights. Despite at least partial vic-
tories in each of these efforts, political forces during the 1980s
were as damaging to unions as economic changes. Under Reagan
the National Labor Relations Board accelerated its rightward shift
and companies felt increasingly free to permanently replace strik-
ers and to harass and fire union activists among their employees.
The increasing dominance of largely nonunion service industries
in the U.S. economy also cut into the ranks of organized labor.
The proportion of U.S. nonfarm employees holding union cards
fell from 31 percent in 1970 to roughly 16 percent in 1991.[108]

Pressured on all sides, U.S. labor was in no condition to take
on the powerful business interests arrayed in support of free
trade. So while they vigorously pushed their friends in Congress
to just say 'no' to NAFTA, union leaders also sought to join forces
with other NAFTA opponents. Unions took a small step toward
adopting a broader social agenda—a direction that progressive activists had long been advocating—by finding allies among environmental activists and consumer advocates. These two groups
enjoyed strong support in many western states and among upper-
middle-class citizens, complementing labor's working-class base
of support in the Midwest and Northeast.

The proposal for North American free trade also forced a long-
overdue effort to strengthen relations between unionists in the
United States and Mexico. NAFTA presents a common challenge to
U.S. and Mexican labor by pitting workers on either side of the border in close competition for investment capital. This competition
compels workers on both sides to accept unfavorable contracts, ex-
acerbating the downward pressure on wages and benefits that has
characterized the global economy since the 1970s.

To varying degrees U.S. unions and the AFL-CIO began to
reshape their international strategies as well as their domestic
political work. A number of people within U.S. labor recognized
that building an international coalition of unions and other activist organizations spanning the vast gulf between poor and rich
nations should be an essential part of labor's response to NAFTA
and to economic globalization. The AFL-CIO, several individual

unions, and a number of small, labor-based groups have taken the first steps in this direction. After years of neglect they are seeking out Mexican counterparts to develop joint strategies and cooperative projects, and to improve communication and understanding.

Given the history of cross-border relations, however, both Mexican and U.S. unions have proceeded cautiously. In many cases, a lack of knowledge about complex labor and political issues in each country hinders effective cross-border work. Worker-to-worker exchanges, conferences, and other opportunities to meet and discuss problems and solutions are helping to overcome these barriers and establish links between counterparts. Such exchanges play a crucial role in enhancing rank-and-file understanding of the process of globalization and add a human significance to calls for international solidarity.

Cross-border worker-to-worker exchanges have grown exponentially after a group called Mujer a Mujer (Woman to Woman) began sponsoring visits by Mexican unionists to the United States in 1985. Likewise, a small, New York-based group called Mexico-U.S. Diálogos has sponsored a series of bi- and trinational exchanges that started in 1988. Bringing together North American counterparts from different social sectors, these events provide a forum for activists to share perspectives and explore goals and strategies.

Other U.S. unions have made contacts through efforts to link NAFTA opponents across North America.[109] At an October 1991 trinational anti-NAFTA meeting in Zacatecas, Mexico, for example, United Electrical Workers (UE) representatives met officials of the Authentic Labor Front (FAT). The two groups have since embarked on the most concrete example of labor solidarity to date, agreeing to cooperate in organizing maquiladora workers. The effort is focusing on "runaway" plants that started up in Mexico after shutting down UE-represented shops in the United States.

ACTWU has actively promoted worker-to-worker exchanges and has begun to share information about specific companies with several Mexican labor organizations, including some independent groups. "We're talking with anybody we can talk with" in Mexico, said ACTWU research director Ron Blackwell. In some cases the talking includes programmatic work, potentially involving joint campaigns targeting specific companies. Several locals of the Service Employees International Union have traveled to Mexico to meet with counterparts. Representatives of Local 790 in San

Francisco were impressed with opposition party leader Cuauhtémoc Cárdenas—an ally of FAT—and sent observers to monitor state-level elections in Michoacán in 1992.

In another example of nascent cross-border cooperation, the Communications Workers of America (CWA) and the Communications and Electrical Workers of Canada signed a "strategic alliance" in early 1992 with the Mexican Telephone Workers Union—a "modernizing" union that strongly supports NAFTA.[110] The agreement is more of a confidence-building measure that could lead to greater future involvement than a specific commitment to joint action. The three signatories committed themselves to "the permanent exchange of trade union information" and, "when necessary and possible," to "support joint mobilization."[111]

As these examples show, once the networks of labor unions in each country have been established, coordinated bargaining strategies and joint actions become more feasible. The effort to forge international alliances faces serious obstacles, however. For one thing, Mexican unions are somewhat skeptical of the new cross-border initiatives. From their perspective, U.S. labor has been at times arrogant, ignorant, and racist in its relations with Mexican unions and workers. For decades the AFL-CIO's support for U.S. business expansion abroad and its active role in undermining independent union movements fueled alienation and suspicion among Mexican unionists, especially among the independent factions that would be needed as allies in the fight against the ill effects of globalization.

One effect of this skepticism may have been the limited Mexican participation in the Coalition for Justice in the Maquiladoras, which lists only two Mexican organizations as members. The AFL-CIO's central role in organizing and funding the coalition made some Mexican organizations wary of its purposes. In at least one case a U.S. group turned down the coalition's invitation to join for fear of damaging its working relations with Mexican counterparts.

According to a close observer of the efforts to forge cross-border labor links, a Mexican union leader recently asked his U.S. counterpart, "Why, all of a sudden, are you calling us 'brothers'? Is it because today you realize you need us, because you are about to lose your jobs—even perhaps your unions—and because you think we stand to gain from your loss? Where have you been for the past forty years, when many times we were in need of you?"[112]

The fact that a gain for Mexican workers might indeed be a loss for U.S. workers also hinders better U.S.-Mexican union relations. Mexican unions have largely supported NAFTA, agreeing with their country's president that a free trade pact is likely to attract foreign investors to Mexico and, therefore, to increase employment. It is difficult, however, to judge the sincerity of Mexican unions' support for free trade due to the dependence of labor leaders on the ruling party.[113]

This dependence poses yet another serious obstacle to cross-border labor cooperation. Most Mexican unions are formally affiliated with the ruling Institutional Revolutionary Party (PRI), which has a corporatist structure that links the "official" labor unions, peasant associations, and other important sectoral groups directly to the decision-making centers of the government. The PRI allocates a portion of its congressional seats and an occasional governorship to leaders of the official unions, and uses their workplace and community networks to get out the vote in support of the party at election time. Until 1991 the collective bargaining agreements of official unions required union members to join the PRI. This "forced mass affiliation" of workers has ended on paper, but local union leaders still put great pressure on their members to sign up with the PRI. Local union leaders who fail to deliver votes are unlikely to climb the promotional ladder.[114]

Even more important to the system than getting out the vote is the role of official unions in ensuring labor's cooperation with the government's economic programs. During the economic crisis from 1982 to 1987, for instance, Mexico's labor leaders opposed the government's severe austerity programs in their speeches, but they failed to mobilize workers to protest the policies. Mexican workers suffered accordingly: The real minimum wage was cut roughly in half during this period.

Since 1987 the government has signed a series of tripartite "economic pacts" with labor and business representatives.[115] The pacts spell out the government's policies regarding peso devaluation, subsidies, and prices for state services and products. Business representatives pledge to respect price hike limits, and labor leaders agree to a cap on wage hikes. In every pact the negotiated increase in the minimum wage has lagged behind inflation.

Mexico's state-labor relationship is a very effective system of social control, a fact that works against transboundary organizing and U.S.-Mexican labor solidarity. The foundation of this system is the government's authority to disapprove union applications for legal recognition, to declare strikes illegal, and to resolve intraunion disputes, including overseeing union elections. Where two unions compete to represent one workplace the government can tilt the balance toward the union it favors. In some cases the government has encouraged cooperative unions to challenge more assertive ones to force the existing union to change its strategy or to replace the union altogether.[116] Where dissident unionists challenge docile leaders, the state can stack the deck heavily in favor of the leaders.

The government prefers not to intervene in labor disputes too often. It therefore allows union bosses to maintain nearly authoritarian control over their organizations—as long as they continue to support the PRI and the government's policies. The "elected" leaders of union locals have nearly unlimited power to revoke the union membership of individual workers. This is a powerful lever of control over local dissidents, since an employer is usually required to fire any workers who lose their union membership. (Corporate managers often find it easier to pay off a corrupt union head to revoke the membership of a trouble-making worker than to fire the worker directly.) Unless the government desires to "get" a given union by scrutinizing its practices, anything goes in elections for local union leaders, including voting by nonmembers, explicit threats that a wrong vote will cost workers their jobs, the requirement that workers sign their ballots, and violence committed by hired thugs.

The state-dominated labor system benefits corporations at the expense of workers. It also encourages the kind of worker repression that NAFTA opponents fear will increase in the absence of explicit, enforceable protections for labor. But those who profit from the system express few concerns about issues like these. For example, Nicholas Scheele, director of Ford Motor Company's Mexican operations, commended the Mexican labor system. "It's very easy to look at this in simplistic terms and say this is wrong," he said, referring to official union corruption. "But is there any other country in the world where the working class . . . took a hit in their purchasing power of in excess of 50 percent over an eight-year period and you didn't have social revolution?"[117]

In addition to building direct contacts and forging joint strategies with cross-border counterparts, a second international labor strategy involves the establishment of enforceable minimum labor standards. Enforcing existing laws is a first step in this process. In the United States, this means using the provisions of the 1984 Trade and Tariff Act that require countries to meet internationally recognized minimum labor standards in order to gain duty-free access to the U.S. market for their goods.

In 1991 a group of U.S. activists filed a petition with the Office of the U.S. Trade Representative (USTR) requesting that Mexican exports be denied eligibility for duty-free treatment, based on the violation of workers' rights at the Ford plant in Cuautitlán, among other items. The USTR rejected the petition out of hand, illegally failing to detail its reasons. "How do you overlook the fact that Mexican workers are routinely fired, beaten, disappeared, shot, and even killed for exercising their right to democratic trade unionism?" asked petitioner and Ford worker Tom Laney in a "reminder letter" to USTR Carla Hills. "The only reason for their rejection I can think of is that it would mess up their negotiations of NAFTA," he said.[118]

The trade office's rejection of the petition highlighted the difficulty of relying on individual nations to enforce international labor rights. The process as it is now structured is hostage to the political priorities of the executive branch. But labor-rights activists argue that only by bringing cases, filing suits, and demonstrating the system's ineffectiveness will they be able to force the issue onto the national agenda. And only by working closely with labor organizations around the globe will activists be able to build trust, incorporate concerns, and create an international movement to include labor rights in international trade and investment agreements.

This is an area ripe for U.S.-Mexican labor cooperation. Such issues as occupational health and safety, the rights to bargain collectively and to strike without being fired, and the enforcement of child labor laws are issues on which both sides should be able to agree. The debate over NAFTA provides a platform for raising labor standards in policy circles, even if NAFTA itself appears unlikely to be modified. "We're meeting . . . with people from Mexico and Canada to discuss parallel talks, where we'll develop counterproposals to put before Congress," according to ACTWU's Blackwell.

Much trickier, however, and more important in the long run, is the question of how to guarantee that workers are free to join the union of their choice and to elect their leaders democratically. Working toward these goals may well mean that U.S. labor will have to weaken or sever its ties with official Mexican unions. It almost certainly means providing moral and material support to independent unions in Mexico and applying strong political pressure in the United States.

But U.S. unions must also strengthen their own positions through grassroots organizing, democratize their own internal structures, and learn to think on a consistently global plane. "Corporations already make plans and build alliances as though national borders were not even there," notes Joe Fahey, president of Teamsters Local 912, which lost hundreds of jobs when its Green Giant plant ran away to cheaper pastures in Mexico. "Labor has a long way to go to catch up."[119]

Chapter 4

Free Trade:
The Ifs, Ands, & Buts

In 1990 the term *free trade* slipped out of economics textbooks and into the everyday conversation of Mexicans and Americans when Presidents Salinas and Bush agreed to initiate negotiations leading to a regional free trade agreement. Canada joined the talks in 1991, and after more than a year of intense negotiations, the leaders of the three countries signed the North American Free Trade Agreement in December 1992. At the insistence of newly elected U.S. President Bill Clinton, in 1993 the parties added two "side agreements" concerning the enforcement of environmental and labor laws. By the fall of that year each administration had placed implementation of the accord in the hands of its national legislature.

NAFTA called for the elimination of all tariffs and import quotas among the three countries within fifteen years.[120] It subjected nontariff trade barriers, such as product safety standards, to the decisions of a trinational panel of judges. By lowering barriers to trade NAFTA promised to facilitate the flow of goods and services within the region. But more than a trade agreement, NAFTA encouraged increased cross-border investment by requiring that foreign investors be given the same rights and opportunities as domestic investors, except in a few economic sectors such as the media and the petroleum industry.

Actually NAFTA spelled out no major changes in U.S. or Canadian policies toward trade and investment. Although the agreement required more changes in Mexican policies, there were only a few changes that the country had not already made or was not planning to make with or without it. In all three countries, NAFTA represented just another step down the road toward global economic integration. For the most part, this economic liberalization had been occurring within the context of the multilateral General Agreement on Tariffs and Trade (GATT). But the free trade bandwagon had also been pushed forward by bilateral "framework agreements" on trade that Washington had been promoting since the early 1980s.

Free trade with Canada had been a sleeper of an issue with the general U.S. public. But free trade with Mexico ignited large-scale public debate. More than a discussion of the specific provisions of NAFTA, the debate revolved around broader economic and social questions. Would freer trade generate prosperity as promised or lead to further economic decline? Would further trade and investment liberalization limit the ability of nations to adopt their own industrial policies and development strategies? Was free trade nothing more than a corporate bill of rights that ignored the basic needs and social values of citizens? And finally, what alternatives are there to the agenda represented by NAFTA and GATT in a world increasingly shaped by the forces of global integration of finance and production?

The Ideal and Reality of Free Trade

Free trade is a powerful ideal that has guided many economists and policy makers since the 1700s. It conjures a vision of a harmonious international system in which goods flow as freely among nations as they do among the states of the United States of America. With no tariff barriers, no quotas, and no customs inspections to impede products or services as they cross national boundaries, market forces are able to allocate resources among all nations in a way that eventually maximizes everyone's income. Free trade would allow consumers in each country to benefit from the skills and resources of others, businesspeople to earn top dollar on their investments, and workers to enjoy the fruits of their ever more productive labor.

Undergirding this vision of trade-induced prosperity is classic free market economic theory, which postulates that economies grow most rapidly when markets are unfettered by artificial barriers such as government regulations. Taken to its logical extreme, free trade ties national economies so closely together that they operate as a single, global economy. But where trade barriers divide national markets, it is the theory of comparative advantage that supports the assertion that lowering the barriers creates greater wealth for all parties. Introducing the theory in 1817, British economist David Ricardo demonstrated that if England could produce textiles more efficiently than it could produce wine, and if Portugal could produce wine more efficiently than it could cloth, both countries would benefit from trading textiles for wine. In more general terms, Ricardo's models showed that global welfare would increase if all nations specialized in making those goods that they could produce most efficiently and then traded freely among themselves.

The free trade vision of Ricardo and his latter-day followers is beautiful in its simplicity and breathtaking in its scope and implications. But like the free market economic model of which it is an extension, free trade works far better on paper than in practice.[121] Indeed, free trade theory suffers from some of the same problems that afflict free market theory, such as the tendency for markets to become dominated by a handful of huge firms, rather than remaining truly competitive.

Many of the problems with the free trade ideal have to do with the assumptions that form its foundation. Free trade theory is based on the lack of government interference in international markets. It assumes that the governments of trading partners are much the same in that they serve the general welfare of their citizens and adhere to the principles of free and competitive markets.

But such assumptions clash with the ways of the real world. Rather than being neutral overseers, governments generally respond to the interests of a domestic elite and work to enhance national power. They use export subsidies to help domestic firms penetrate foreign markets, currency devaluations to lower the cost of exports and raise the cost of imports, public money to fund private research, government procurement to promote critical industries, and mercantilist policies to build large trade surpluses. According to free market theory, each of these policies reduces economic efficiency and thus the overall welfare of the countries that pursue them. Yet governments adopt them both to gain advantages over other nations and to satisfy important domestic constituencies.

Furthermore, not all societies have the same understanding of social welfare. And much of what goes into the concept is difficult or impossible to include in economic calculations. Nations create laws and institutions that distort markets to accomplish differing social goals, such as national security, a healthy population, a clean environment, equitable income sharing, and cultural preservation.

Were government barriers to trade suddenly to be removed from the real economy, rather than from mathematical models, the differences in national goals and values would translate into serious trade conflicts. Countries with economically inefficient but socially valuable policies would find themselves disadvantaged relative to others that made economic efficiency their first priority. Governments that followed a laissez-faire strategy would find their nation's firms suffering at the hands of governments that provided subsidies or other assistance to their corporations. To minimize the conflicts likely to arise from such a trading system, governments must negotiate the rules under which economic integration will occur.

But the very fact that free trade must be negotiated makes achieving the free trade ideal unlikely in the real world. Negotiators come to the table with vastly different resources and needs. Those with greater resources and fewer needs have the power to bend the terms of a trade agreement in their favor, resulting in an uneven playing field.

These real-world obstacles to implementing free trade have been around for centuries. The last three decades have seen another, more fundamental problem arise that renders the basis of free trade theory obsolete. When Ricardo developed the theory of comparative advantage, a country's capital and technology were nearly as fixed as its land. But both now cross national borders at will, and modern corporations can establish operations in most parts of the world. No longer can a country rely on its capital base and technological lead to give it a trade advantage.

Despite its appeal to mainstream economic theoreticians, until World War II almost all nations rejected the idea of lowering their own tariff walls and other trade barriers, believing that free trade would give an unfair advantage to the trading partner with the most advanced industrial base. As the dominant industrial power until the early 1900s, Britain stood alone in its push for free trade. Britain's trading partners, including the United States, rejected its overtures, preferring to help their industries develop behind protective trade walls.

While largely refusing to lower their own tariffs on imports from competing countries, the world's imperial powers often used the banner of free trade to justify military campaigns to open up the markets and natural resources of the world's less developed nations. The colonial trading blocs that resulted led to conflicts between the major industrial powers over access to markets and raw materials. Escalating protectionism and disputes over discriminatory trade practices were major causes of two world wars in the twentieth century.

Without its own colonial system to serve as an outlet for goods and a source of supplies, the United States has historically been a leading proponent of open global markets. The country appealed to this principle to justify going to war in 1898 with Spain, claiming that Spanish mercantilism was obstructing the free flow of trade and colonial institutions were retarding the development of democracy. World War II and the disastrous experience of the United States' own protectionist measures in the 1930s reinforced the free trade position.

World War II placed the United States in a position of uncontested economic dominance, from which it was able to push its European allies to gradually open their markets. With its capitalist allies in tow, the United States sought to establish a new, conflict-free trading regime that would lower tariff barriers and regulate trade by establishing rules of fair play. In 1944 the governments created the International Monetary Fund (IMF) to stabilize currency markets and to monitor domestic economic policies. In 1947, overruling a European proposal for a more managed system of world trade, the United States convinced its allies to approve the GATT. The IMF and especially GATT not only would facilitate larger trade flows in the short term, they would ensure that economic liberalization remained high on the global agenda for decades.

GATT and the IMF were designed by the industrialized market economies to serve their own interests, and they ignored the needs of developing countries until the mid-1960s. Beginning in the 1970s and accelerating in the 1980s, both institutions came to play a central role in the capitalist North's effort to steer developing countries away from state-directed development strategies such as import-substituting industrialization and toward closer integration into the international market economy. Assisted by the globalization of production and finance and the growing domination of transnational corporations, free trade advocates began to press developing countries to sign on to GATT and to limit governmental interference with markets.

Espousing the principles of economic liberalism of the 1700s, neoliberals today argue that developing countries need to embrace free trade because the gains from trade between poor and wealthy countries could be far greater than those from trade among the industrialized nations. This is because the products of wealthy economies generally incorporate similar resources—capital, technology, and skilled labor—so that what one country exports often could as easily be made in the importing industrial country. But poor countries' exports are likely to embody different resources—unskilled labor and raw materials—that will complement those of wealthy countries and create gains from specialization and trade, according to the theory of comparative advantage.

In the case of North America, Mexico's relatively high ratio of workers to good farmland is said to give it a comparative advantage in "labor-intensive" agricultural goods—those that involve much manual labor, such as vegetables and fruits. Mexico also has a relatively high ratio of low-skilled workers to capital, giving it a comparative advantage in low-technology, labor-intensive manufacturing.

As Mexico opens trade with a capital-abundant country like the United States, the theory holds that Mexico will be able to sell more of the labor-intensive products it makes to the United States and will buy more of the capital-intensive products that U.S. firms produce. Under free trade Mexican workers will benefit from the increased demand for their labor, as will skilled workers producing high-technology goods and services in the United States. Capitalists in the United States will also gain from the wider range of investment opportunities and increased demand in Mexico for their capital, and consumers in both countries will in theory have more options and lower prices.

The Goals of Regional Free Trade

Embracing the ideals of free trade, the concept of a North American free trade region won the backing of all three of the area's governments by early 1991. What was so striking was not that Canada and the United States—two developed nations of the North—should join in a free trade agreement but that the less developed Mexico would be included as an equal partner in such an accord. A shared commitment to neoliberal, free market principles united the three countries, but their vast economic and political disparities meant that each country approached NAFTA with different goals.

Mexico looked to a free trade agreement with the United States primarily to attract foreign investment. An injection of dollars and technology would fuel economic growth, pull the country out of the stagnation of the "lost decade" of the 1980s, and help modernize crucial elements of its infrastructure. Mexico needed foreign capital because the nation's debt and its neoliberal economic strategy precluded a large infusion of public investment. Furthermore, Mexican capitalists were unlikely to provide the necessary investment. In some cases, Mexican investors lacked confidence in the staying power of the new probusiness government outlook. More important, they saw a flat domestic market, and with a few exceptions they lacked the technology and distribution networks to penetrate foreign markets. Attracting significant foreign investment to Mexico through free trade would not only help solve these problems but also provide immediate balance-of-payments relief.

Given the country's reputation for sudden policy shifts and the unpredictable nature of presidential succession, increasing investor confidence in the stability of Mexico's economic policy was a crucial part of attracting investment. A formal trade agreement would send a powerful signal to both domestic and foreign investors that Mexico had made a clean break with its history of governmental economic leadership.

A free trade agreement would also serve to enhance Mexico's position as an export platform to the United States, one of the country's major attractions to foreign investors. Rising protectionist sentiment in the United States—although directed mainly against the persistent surpluses of east Asian trading partners—threatened Mexico's access to the U.S. market as well. Already, potentially attractive investment opportunities in several industries—apparel, steel, and some agricultural products—were subject to bilateral or multilateral marketing arrangements that effectively set quotas on U.S. imports. If a free trade agreement exempted Mexico from such restrictions and guaranteed long-term access to U.S. consumers, the country would have a clear leg up on the international competition for export-oriented investment.

Opening Mexico's markets to one of the world's most efficient economies carries significant dangers for domestic businesses. In most sectors those companies least prepared for international competition had already gone bankrupt during the market liberalizations preceding NAFTA. But protection remained in place for a number of industries, topped by the production of basic agricultural goods such as corn, soybeans, sorghum, and beans. Along with agricultural producers, U.S. providers of services from banking and insurance to engineering represented great threats to their Mexican counterparts, and to a lesser extent so did industries such as rubber, plastics, and scientific instruments.

For Washington, too, the free trade proposal offered the opportunity to achieve multiple objectives. In strictly economic terms it presented the chance to open the door to Mexico's long-protected market even wider than it had been opened by the country's drive to liberalize trade and to give U.S. products an edge over those produced in Japan or Europe. Although Mexican consumers do not have the buying power to make a significant contribution to the U.S. economy, a decade of rapid economic growth sparked by free trade might change the picture, and an agreement would give U.S.-based producers a head start in meeting that growing demand.[122]

Furthermore, a boom in industrial investment and production would result in greater demand for U.S. products, especially in critical industries like machine tools and information processing, since Mexican industry purchases the large majority of its capital and intermediate goods from U.S. firms. In addition, opening new sectors of Mexico's economy—such as financial services and automobiles—to U.S. exports and investment could boost specific troubled industries in the United States. The gains to many industries exporting to Mexico and to those that would increase their investment in the country—such as financial and telecommunications firms—would more than compensate for losses that could be expected in many protected areas of the U.S. economy, free trade advocates claimed.[123]

Beyond its own economic reasons, the United States had long sought to ensure that its southern neighbor remained politically stable, even when Mexican leaders attacked the United States rhetorically. A free trade accord could accomplish this, U.S. strategists reasoned, both by aiding a friendly administration and by supporting Mexico's neoliberal economic strategy. Economic growth would also reduce the flow of Mexican migrants seeking a better life north of the border, according to reports by numerous commissions over the years.[124]

Washington also saw an opportunity to use free trade with Mexico as a springboard for its hemispheric free trade aspirations. NAFTA could serve as a model for multilateral trade agreements with other countries of the Americas, establishing precedents viewed as crucial by Washington, such as equal treatment of foreign and domestic investors and strong protection of intellectual property rights. Some observers suggested that NAFTA could even serve as the mechanism by which the free trade component of Bush's Enterprise for the Americas Initiative would be implemented, since provisions in NAFTA allowed additional countries to "accede" to the pact by negotiating with the Free Trade Commission it established.[125]

Canada had little choice but to join the talks. Having already opened its markets to U.S. corporations with the U.S.-Canada Free Trade Agreement in 1988, the country faced having to share the preferential access to the U.S. market it had gained in exchange. Automobiles and petroleum give Canada its $14 billion trade surplus with the United States, and both are top Mexican exports to the United States as well. Furthermore, Canadian corporations in capital-goods and other high-technology industries feared ceding the potentially important Mexican market to their U.S. competitors if Canada stayed out of NAFTA. To defend its interests as best it could, Canada asked to join the negotiations in February 1991.[126]

NAFTA represented an attempt to shape economic integration along neoliberal lines, using trade as a lever to limit government's ability to interfere with business priorities. Lowering barriers to trade and investment necessarily involves raising barriers to governments' ability to regulate those flows. The North American trading partners of the United States sought precisely this effect in signing on to free trade. According to former Canadian trade negotiator Michael Hart, a key goal for Canada in NAFTA was "to further lock in the market orientation of the Canadian economy."[127] President Salinas and his top aides made clear on several occasions that a free trade agreement would attract foreign investment to Mexico by increasing the likelihood that his successors will continue his probusiness policies.

In accordance with free trade theory, proponents of NAFTA believe that leaving as much decision-making power as possible to markets and the private sector will result in an efficient regional economy and rapid growth, especially in less developed Mexico. Furthermore, economic growth will then create the wealth and political stability needed to enhance the enforcement of environmental and labor laws.

No Longer a Theoretical Debate

The debate over NAFTA that emerged in the United States and Canada was essentially the same one building about the direction of free trade initiatives within GATT. On the one hand, labor organizations and certain business sectors are concerned that unregulated trade and investment flows, especially between such unequal partners as the United States and Mexico, will mean that jobs and industries will be lost and there will be a downward pressure on wages. On the other hand, environmentalists and consumer advocates felt that the health, safety, and conservation standards they had worked hard to achieve would be endangered by free trade agreements that emphasize business over people and environment. In both cases, opponents called for their governments to protect living standards and social values from what they feared would be the "downward harmonization" caused by the leveling force of free trade.

In Mexico, objections to the free trade deal were not as widespread, although public opinion surveys showed that opposition to NAFTA was significant and growing. Many businesses feared they would be overrun by U.S. goods and investment. The PRI's influence over the media and the national congress greatly restricted the breadth of the debate over free trade in Mexico.[128] But a genuine desire on the part of Mexicans for drastic economic change also explained the lack of a strong popular opposition. Many Mexicans appeared to have chosen the promise of new jobs and economic growth resulting from closer links with the world's largest economy over traditional nationalistic concerns about the Colossus of the North.

Most opposition in Mexico focused on issues of sovereignty and self-determination, and on the lack of democratic process. Historian Lorenzo Meyer declared that "our way of life is at stake."

Similarly, a columnist normally supportive of Salinas observed that an agreement would result not in integration but in the "annexation" of Mexico.[129] Such statements express the deep concern that by adopting free trade and hitching its future to the U.S. star Mexico would be losing the opportunity to determine its own economic and political future. Would Mexico become just another Puerto Rico, totally dependent on the whims of U.S. investors and forever denied the potential of embracing a development model different from one dictated by the needs of the U.S. economy?

In all three countries opponents argued that NAFTA should be linked to social and environmental issues and pointed to the rules governing the European common market as a model. Starting as they did from a more regulated capitalism, the member nations of the European Community understood that the effects of integration reach well beyond strict economics and accepted the need for a significant government role in managing that integration for the greater good. They therefore included rules covering migration and environmental and labor standards, a managed agricultural policy, and a European Parliament in the process.[130] NAFTA, on the other hand, focused almost exclusively on business issues. Although it allows countries to impose minimum standards on the safety and cleanliness of imports, NAFTA ignored labor rights, work standards, and pollution-abatement goals.

Despite negotiators' efforts to present NAFTA as a business-only pact, free trade agreements are inherently about more than economics. What to include to ensure that all parties benefit in the long term, what restrictions to place on government policy making, and what institutions to establish to carry the integrative process forward through the decades are fundamentally political questions; the answers to those questions help determine who has what power within society.

NAFTA opponents argued that the agreement had been designed to give a great deal of power to corporations, and they feared that if it were approved it would lock in a probusiness bent to all three countries' domestic policies. The pact could not accomplish these objectives merely by stipulating what governments can and cannot do, since future leaders could abrogate the agreement—albeit at some political cost. The staying power of an agreement like NAFTA stems from the fact that the economies of the three countries will gradually be restructured to reflect the integrated continental market. Firms will make production and investment decisions based on unrestricted access to consumers, workers, investors, and other resources of the three countries. After a decade of such private sector decisions, pulling out of the agreement would impose large costs on corporations and a country's trade flows. This economic cost, combined with the political fallout caused by angering the corporate elite, would make unilateral changes to or withdrawals from NAFTA highly improbable if and when the agreement was fully implemented.

NAFTA threatened to tie policy makers to a probusiness agenda in a second, subtler way. Without safeguards along the lines of those included in the European Community's plan for integration, competitiveness becomes the bottom-line consideration for all national and international policies. The deregulatory drive of the Reagan and Bush administrations provided a preview of the competitiveness effect. Citing concern for the international competitiveness of U.S. firms, the two presidents launched an all-out attack on regulations intended to protect workers, consumers, and the environment. In 1990 Bush empowered his Council on Competitiveness—headed by then-Vice President Dan Quayle—to review all new and existing regulations for their "anti-competitive" impact. The council forced changes in EPA regulations, pressed the heads of the U.S. Department of Agriculture and the Food and Drug Administration to reconsider consumer safety rules, and sought to overhaul the nation's civil-justice system to reduce the threat of lawsuits against businesses. In each of these cases the council claimed the regulations cost U.S. businesses money, putting them at a disadvantage vis-à-vis foreign competitors while costing U.S. workers their jobs.[131]

The same deregulatory juggernaut swept through Canada in the wake of its free trade agreement with the United States. The country moved away from its strict standard for pesticide safety toward the weaker U.S. version.[132] Social programs were cut back or attacked, as with unemployment insurance and the minimum wage, both of which were more generous than in the United States.[133] The Canadian Chamber of Commerce challenged its federal and provincial governments to adopt the standard applied by Quayle's council, demanding that "all Canadian governments must test all their policies to determine whether or not they reinforce or impede competitiveness. If a policy is anticompetitive, dump it."[134]

Canadian and U.S. corporations not only pressed their governments for more favorable policies, they used the free trade agreement to attack environmental and other programs through the bilateral commission set up to rule on trade disputes. U.S. firms sued to overturn Canada's efforts to reduce acid rain through subsidized pollution control equipment, claiming the subsidies constituted unfair government assistance. Likewise, Canadian companies attacked the U.S. ban on asbestos, arguing that it illegally blocked their exports to this country.[135]

Such examples illustrated the argument made by many opponents of NAFTA and other free trade initiatives that inattention to social policies leaves open the possibility of competition based on the abuse of workers or the environment. Standards are needed to protect against a downward spiral of deregulation intended to attract industry and give domestic firms cost advantages on the international market, much as the rules of GATT and the IMF were set up to prevent destructive competition based on export subsidies or predatory exchange rate policies. From this perspective the problem with NAFTA and the broader free trade agenda is not the fact that it would set global rules but rather who is setting them—and for whose benefit.

Proponents of a broader trinational agreement point to Europe as evidence that free trade need not take an antiregulatory course. They argue that the United States and its trading partners could adopt the strictest rather than the loosest regulation in any given area, phasing in changes over a decade or so and providing financing for technology transfer and enhanced enforcement. This would level the playing field for businesses, eliminate socially destructive competition, and force companies to compete on the basis of productive factors such as quality, productivity, and innovation.[136]

The conflict between those who approached NAFTA from a purely business perspective and those who preferred these broader approaches to a trade accord encompassed many issues. Two areas that stimulated the most vigorous controversy, however, concerned the trade agreement's potential effects on wages and employment, on the one hand, and the environment on the other. Aside from drawing the most fire, these issues also exemplified the difficulties of establishing a free trade relationship between such markedly unequal partners as the United States and Mexico. For example, questions over which jobs will be lost or gained, how well basic needs will be met by wages and benefits, and how many resources are available for environmental protection illustrate the effects of asymmetry on the relationship as well as the macroeconomic realities faced by each country individually. In addition, these crucial areas highlighted the role played by the U.S. and Mexican governments in shaping the accord to satisfy particular constituencies and to achieve their own political and economic goals.

The Wage and Employment Debate

The Bush, Salinas, and Mulroney administrations campaigned vigorously to convince their publics that North American free trade would create jobs and raise living standards in all three countries, as did the Clinton administration after it entered office.[137] With the three North American administrations all touting the economic benefits of continental free trade, the debate over NAFTA's effect on workers in all three countries took center stage. In the face of the conventional free market arguments advanced by their national leaders and other free trade supporters, U.S. and Canadian opponents of NAFTA contended that the pact would accelerate the deindustrialization of their countries by encouraging firms to move production to Mexico. Investment in the two wealthier countries would slow as capital flowed south, and this would limit the growth of productivity.

In hearings, at rallies, and on television documentaries, blue-collar workers across the United States and Canada expressed fear for their jobs. If their corporate employers did not lay them off in search of higher profits from a cheaper labor force, workers worried, they might do so out of necessity in the face of competition from other companies that did move to Mexico. NAFTA opponents also argued that removing the last barriers to competition with workers in Mexico would dramatically increase the downward pressure on wages, labor rights, and working conditions that U.S. and Canadian workers had been facing since the 1970s.

Canadian workers had already experienced the free trade slide. In the years following the U.S.-Canada Free Trade Agreement, many Canadian manufacturing facilities moved south—to the United States, where wages and labor laws were generally much more favorable to employers than in Canada. According to the Canadian Labour Congress, nearly 250,000 jobs were lost because of the agreement in its first two years.[138] Statistics Canada reports that a total of 461,000 manufacturing jobs vanished between June 1989 and October 1991, representing nearly one-fourth of manufacturing employment.[139] It is difficult to determine how many of these jobs were lost as a direct result of liberalizing trade and investment flows with the United States given the global recession that hit at the same time, but anecdotal evidence and the fact that manufacturing suffered far more in Canada than in the United States indicated that the free trade agreement at least exacerbated the downturn.[140]

Not only do Mexican workers receive far lower wages than their counterparts to the north, but the laws that protect their health and safety as well as those that set maximum work hours and a minimum age limit are commonly ignored. As with other areas of Mexican social standards, the laws are strong—in some cases stronger than those of the United States—but enforcement is spotty. Both in the maquiladoras, the focus of numerous investigations, and in the rest of the economy, which has received far less attention, abuses of occupational safety, overtime, and child labor laws are commonplace.[141]

To minimize the competitive advantage to be gained by abusing these laws, labor activists, children's advocates, and others campaigned to gain assurances within NAFTA that standards in all three countries would be strengthened by the pact. But the three North American administrations refused to include the subject in negotiations. To demonstrate their concern for the issue, however, presidents Bush and Salinas directed their secretaries of labor to negotiate an agreement as NAFTA was being hammered out. The result was a series of studies and seminars emphasizing technical assistance and cooperation but explicitly rejecting the notion of tying labor laws or their enforcement to trading privileges.[142]

Even after President Clinton campaigned to include protections for workers in a side agreement to NAFTA, guarantees of such labor rights as collective bargaining, freedom of association, and information about occupational hazards remained off the table. The side agreement on labor that was signed in September

1993 allowed enforcement through fines or trade sanctions only for violations of individual nations' laws covering minimum wages and maximum work hours. No mechanism was included for raising these or other standards, and the commission that was called for to hear cases was to be composed of government appointees only. Labor unionists and other worker activists vigorously condemned the side agreements as failing to address their concerns with NAFTA.

Labor was not the only group predicting that U.S. industry would pick up stakes and move to Mexico if NAFTA passed. In a *Wall Street Journal* poll of 505 senior executives of U.S. manufacturing companies, 40 percent said it was at least likely that their firms would shift some production to Mexico in the few years following a free trade pact. Not all the new investment would cost jobs in the United States—some firms would shift their Asian operations to Mexico—and some of the movement would occur without NAFTA, but the overall effect was made clear by a follow-up question. Thirty-nine percent of respondents said NAFTA would have a "mostly unfavorable" or "very unfavorable" impact on U.S. workers.[143] Independent presidential candidate H. Ross Perot opposed NAFTA steadfastly, based in part on his informal survey of fifteen executives of top U.S. corporations. All of them, he reported, would locate their next facility in Mexico if NAFTA passed.

Lastly, NAFTA was unlikely to help Mexican workers, according to opponents of the agreement, because it contained no mechanisms that would allow them to resist their government's repressive, low-wage strategy. That strategy had already produced hundreds of thousands of jobs in foreign-owned assembly plants in Mexico. Despite the added employment and the increasing productivity of Mexican workers, their real wages fell by between 20 percent and 40 percent from 1982 to 1991. Nor did the trade agreement include provisions for financing to help Mexico pay off its debt and invest in education, infrastructure, or other projects needed to foster long-term growth.

To help it evaluate the competing claims, the U.S. Congress asked the U.S. International Trade Commission (ITC) to conduct a study of the likely economic effects of a free trade agreement with Mexico. The ITC found that the nation as a whole would benefit slightly, but that unskilled workers "would suffer a slight decline in real income."[144] When pressed to spell out what it meant by "unskilled workers," the ITC revealed that the category included nearly three-quarters of the U.S. work force. A few months later the ITC made a few "minor adjustments" in the data it had used to reach its conclusions and issued a revised report finding that both skilled and unskilled workers would benefit from NAFTA.[145]

Whether or not the ITC's data switch was based on political considerations, the ability of a minor change to significantly alter the results of an economic model demonstrates the importance of examining the assumptions that economic forecasters make. The economic models cited by NAFTA proponents are virtually all based on sophisticated versions of Ricardo's theory of comparative advantage. As did Ricardo, the models assume that wage and price levels are set by the free play of supply and demand in smoothly functioning markets. Although economists know better, they use these models because they do not have the tools to analyze the real economy, and they believe that making a few simplifying assumptions will at least enable them to predict general trends, if not specific outcomes. But if a model starts by assuming full employment and the equations it uses are based on maintaining full employment, it should hardly be a surprise that its results show continued full employment. Under these conditions, jobs merely shift from one area of the economy to another.

It could be very difficult to figure out how these job shifts will take place, so economists assume perfect markets. When demand for a company's products increases thanks to greater exports, it will hire more workers to boost production. In a perfect market the company must offer a wage higher than that paid elsewhere to attract new workers. By doing so it raises the cost of labor for all other companies, forcing less productive firms to lay off workers or even go bankrupt. According to free-market theory, firms will continue to hire workers until the wages they pay equal the value of the increased production contributed by each additional worker. That means that wages will end up closely tied to productivity.

Free trade skeptics offered North America's experience during the 1980s as exhibit number one against these assumptions. Real manufacturing wages in the United States declined 5 to 10 percent even as labor productivity increased.[146] Although the number of jobs in the economy increased by over twenty million during the decade and the unemployment rate fell, workers' incomes barely improved. Manufacturing workers who lost jobs during the decade often could find no new work, and when work was available it paid an average of 10 percent to 15 percent less than their previous wage.[147]

Given the oft-voiced concern that NAFTA would set off a flow of capital from Canada and the United States to Mexico, the most glaring flaw in the economic models supporting the pact was their assumption that U.S. capital stock would be unaffected even as Mexico attracted billions of dollars in new investments. As one economist noted, "That's equivalent to assuming that Mexicans will wake up one morning to find an extra $25 billion in the middle of Main Street."[148]

When one economic model was adapted to take into account an increase in U.S. foreign investment in Mexico, the results it produced changed dramatically, from a finding of a likely small positive effect on U.S. employment to one of a shift of 550,000 U.S. jobs from high-wage to low-wage industries.[149] A study by four economists who used very different assumptions found that NAFTA would cause the loss of between 290,000 and 490,000 U.S. jobs over a decade.[150]

Despite such evidence, the mainstream models designed to predict the effects of NAFTA are based on the theory of comparative advantage and make the assumptions of full employment and perfect markets. Inevitably, the results they spit out "confirm" the theory. A 1991 study by KPMG Peat Marwick found that NAFTA would create 29,800 new jobs in some sectors of the U.S. economy, would cause the loss of 29,800 jobs in others, and would increase real wages by 0.02 to 0.03 percent. A University of Michigan study the same year estimated U.S. job gains in some sectors to be 99,993 as a result of NAFTA, job losses in others to be 99,993, and real wages to increase by 0.2 percent. Such forced symmetry reflects the fantasy of the underlying assumptions: Neither study shows a net gain or loss of jobs since at full employment neither is possible.

At least six other studies were released in 1991 using this methodology, known as computable general equilibrium modeling.[151] Most declined to put specific numbers on job shifts, but all agreed that the United States would gain in capital-intensive areas and Mexico would gain in labor-intensive areas. And they agreed that the jobs gained would be more productive and therefore better-paying than the jobs lost.[152]

Labor advocates questioned whether new jobs would be created in capital-intensive, high-productivity sectors in the United States and Canada. For one thing, they pointed out, the vast majority of new jobs created in the 1980s—when two million manufacturing jobs disappeared—were in low-paying service-sector positions. In addition, there was little guarantee that the capital-intensive, high-technology industries that free traders were banking on would not join their less advanced brethren in moving to Mexico.

By the time Salinas proposed free trade to Bush, there was plentiful evidence that it was not just low-wage, low-skill jobs that were likely to move to Mexico. Workers in the United States began to face competition from low-paid workers in increasingly high-skill industries, challenging a tenet of the theory of comparative advantage. Often the competition facing U.S. workers was from foreign subsidiaries of their own firms. In 1983 the Ford Motor Company set up a state-of-the-art engine plant in Chihuahua, Mexico, that directly competed with a Ford plant in the United States. With wages less than one-tenth of those in the northern plants, the only question was whether inexperienced Mexican workers could operate the robots efficiently and achieve high-quality standards. Within thirty months the Mexican plant had proved that it was comparable in both respects to the U.S. plant.[153]

Examples of high-quality, high-tech production by low-paid workers on the U.S.-Mexican border have multiplied. From super-clean rooms and surface-mount technology in advanced electronics production to flexible manufacturing systems for automobiles, corporations have found that it pays to set up shop in Mexico. That firms are sending advanced production to Mexico defies conventional economic wisdom, which holds that market forces will allocate labor-intensive, low-productivity work to a low-wage, underskilled country like Mexico. It also belies the sanguine pronouncements of free-market economists that plant shutdowns, including runaways, were a sign of a healthy U.S. economy shedding undesirable activities to make room for new, more valuable ones. Clearly, NAFTA threatened not just low-wage, "undesirable" jobs, but the more advanced, high-technology jobs the Bush and Clinton administrations were counting on. More and more U.S. workers find themselves wondering what will prevent *their* jobs from moving to Mexico. This worry is echoed by members of the communities that depend on those workers' wages.

Evidence that advanced production can be shifted to Mexico gives employers a big stick in contract negotiations with workers. The threat of relocation and the loss of jobs when plants do move away drive wages down. Fully one-quarter of the executives surveyed by *The Wall Street Journal* acknowledged that they would be likely or somewhat likely to use NAFTA as a bargaining lever to hold down wages.[154] According to an economist at the University of California, Los Angeles, increased competition from Mexican workers will depress the wages of unskilled workers in the United States by an estimated one thousand dollars per year.[155]

In the mid-1980s General Motors' Packard Electric Division told its union local in Cleveland, Ohio, that workers would have to accept a 62 percent pay cut for new hires or their jobs would go to Mexico. Packard had no trouble backing up the threat, since GM already employed tens of thousands of workers in Mexico at $1.00 per hour and less. When negotiations ended, the union had a small victory: the pay cut was only 43 percent. In Centralia, Ontario, Fleck Manufacturing carried out the threat: Only hours after its work force went on strike the plant closed down and moved to Ciudad Juárez, Mexico.

Under free trade, wages have a long way yet to fall. Acknowledging the effect of global integration, a Goodyear executive vice-president said that "until we get real wage levels down much closer to those of the Brazils and Koreas, we cannot pass along productivity gains to wages and still be competitive."[156]

Free Trade, the Environment, and the Consumer

Efforts to protect health and environment have in recent years clashed with the free trade agenda. On a global level, these conflicts have increasingly occurred within GATT and have come under consideration for the first time by the Organization for Economic Cooperation and Development (OECD) and the United Nations Conference on Environment and Development (UNCED). On a regional level, the tension between free trade principles and regulations safeguarding the environment and consumers has surfaced within the European Community and as part of the NAFTA negotiating process.

Environmentalists and consumer advocates have been pushing since the 1970s for international agreements and standards on such matters as endangered species protection, deforestation, and ozone control.[157] But it was not until 1990 that these groups made strong demands that the links between international trade and environmental and consumer issues be directly addressed as part of global and regional trade negotiations.

For too long, environmental and safety concerns have been considered merely obstacles to the free flow of goods, services, and investment. At the heart of the environment and trade debate are national or local regulations that protect the environment or consumer safety but also function as nontariff trade barriers. Issues of sovereignty and extraterritoriality also arise in the intensifying debate about the place of environmental and consumer issues in free trade negotiations. Unregulated trade would restrict a nation's ability to manage and conserve its own resources. Nations that adopt measures to preserve the family farm or to control the sale of timber, for example, could be faulted for resorting to unfair trade practices. Free trade agreements could also be used to block trade from nations with production processes that are harmful either to the environment or workers, such as drift-net fishing or the widespread use of child labor. In this sense, a lack of environmental regulations or insufficient enforcement of such regulations by exporting countries could be considered hidden trade subsidies.

Another contentious issue that must be resolved in free trade talks is the role of international standards for consumer products and the environment. It might seem that international standards set by the United Nations or some other global forum would be the ideal solution to resolve differences between trading nations. But although such international standards may represent an upward harmonization for less developed nations, they frequently represent a downward harmonization for industrialized countries with more advanced consumer and environmental regulations.

During 1990, as the Uruguay Round of the GATT entered what was expected to be its final year, these and other environmental/consumer concerns were raised for the first time.[158] In 1971 GATT had established a Group on Environmental Measures and International Trade, but it was not until 1991 that the rules committee was convened.[159] When the United States entered into free trade negotiations with Canada in 1986 the major U.S. environmental and consumer organizers showed little interest. The NAFTA negotiations, however, awakened great concern that regional integration under the banner of free trade was directly threatening the viability of U.S. environmental and health standards.

For many within the environmental community, alarm bells began ringing in early 1991 when a GATT dispute panel ruled in favor of a Mexican complaint that the United States could not fairly ban the importation of Mexican tuna. The United States, acting on the provisions of the Marine Mammal Protection Act, had prohibited the purchase of Mexican tuna on the grounds that Mexican tuna-fishing methods were killing substantial numbers of dolphins.[160] Environmentalists also became alarmed by new reports about environmental degradation along the U.S.-Mexico border. The fact that industries had begun using the 1988 U.S.-Canada Free Trade Agreement to challenge environmental standards and programs in both countries also increased environmental and consumer interest in international trade negotiations.

Recognizing that free trade talks represented the largest and most immediate threat to national and global efforts to protect the environment and citizen welfare, such groups as the Natural Resources Defense Council, Sierra Club, and Public Citizen dramatically increased their attention to international trade issues. Fair trade suddenly became the rallying call not only for labor and leftists who had long been questioning the direction of economic globalization but also for environmentalists and consumer advocates.

Environmentalist pressure did succeed in forcing GATT to consider the trade and environment connection for the first time, but it never became an integral issue within the Uruguay Round. With NAFTA the environmental community was more successful. Trade's impact on the environment and to a lesser degree on consumer health and safety became prominent issues in the NAFTA debate. The relegation of environment to a "parallel track" in the negotiations frustrated environmentalists.[161] But because of their continuing pressure, the final NAFTA draft proved to be an improvement over the 1991 draft of the Uruguay Round (known as the "Dunkel Draft"), which had come under sharp criticism from environmental and consumer organizations.

The trade treaty signed in December 1992 was, in the words of EPA Administrator William Reilly, "the greenest trade treaty ever."[162] Most critics of the free trade proposal acknowledged the truth of that assessment, but noted that previous trade agreements had virtually ignored environmental concerns. In response to concerns raised by environmental and consumer organizations, NAFTA contained provisions that reduced the threat that domestic health and environmental standards would be automatically challenged as constituting nontariff barriers. Standards set by local, state, or national governments could only be challenged if they were designed primarily to block trade.

Rather than define consumer and environmental regulations as trade barriers, the agreement specified that such regulations would not be considered unnecessary barriers to trade if they have a legitimate objective and do not discriminate against particular countries. Among the legitimate objectives specified in the 1992 NAFTA proposal were measures to promote the interests of safety; human, animal, and plant life and health; environment; consumers; and sustainable development. However, the pact limits each party's protection of human, animal, and plant life to that within its own boundaries. A Canadian law intended to conserve Mexico's biodiversity would thus appear to be illegitimate under NAFTA.

Without requiring upward harmonization of standards, as many environmentalists and citizen groups had been advocating, the agreement stated that free trade should occur without reducing environmental and consumer safeguards even if they were stricter in one country than another. In an important departure from GATT, where the burden of proof in disputes over nontariff barriers lies with the defending nation, the proposed NAFTA stated that the party challenging an environmental or consumer measure would have to prove that the defending country's regulation is inconsistent with the agreement.

Two other areas where the final draft showed improvement over earlier drafts concerned scientific justification and risk assessment of environmental and consumer measures. Although still ambiguous, the 1992 agreement appeared only to require that some scientific basis exist to support the formulation of these measures. Rather than insisting on risk/benefit analysis to justify environmental and consumer trade restrictions, the agreement instead stated that these measures be based on risk assessment and merely specified that each party "should take into account the objective of minimizing negative trade effects" in establishing food safety levels. Risk assessment is defined simply as an evaluation of potential adverse effects rather than a judgment that would also consider the economic costs and benefits of these measures.

Measures specifying "zero tolerance" for carcinogens would probably meet the obligation for risk assessment but might not be considered valid when employing risk/benefit analysis.[163]

In late 1993 the trinational Agreement on Environmental Cooperation, signed as a supplemental accord to NAFTA, brought many of the major U.S. environmental organizations on board in favor of NAFTA. These included the National Wildlife Federation, Conservation International, Natural Resources Defense Council, World Wildlife Fund, National Audubon Society, and Environmental Defense Fund. These environmental groups supported NAFTA not only because of new governmental commitments to pollution prevention, but also because they believed that NAFTA would open new channels of communication with Mexico over natural resource conservation and environmental protection. In her public endorsement of NAFTA, Kathryn Fuller, president of the World Wildlife Fund, noted that Mexico has more biological resources than almost any other country and that by acquiring greater economic opportunity through the trade agreement, Mexico would have more money available to protect the environment.[164]

Although gratified that their lobbying and organizing had some success, many other environmentalist groups, including the Sierra Club, Friends of the Earth, and Greenpeace, remained critical of NAFTA as a model for international trade. One objection focused on the accord's failure to promote sustainable development, a concept whose goals include natural resource conservation, biological and cultural diversity, and equity. Although NAFTA listed the promotion of sustainable development as one of its objectives and defined it as a legitimate purpose for environmental regulations, it did not explicitly link trade and the environment. Addressing this link is crucial to achieving sustainable development, these environmentalists argue. An increasingly influential sector of the environmental movement also questions what free trade advocates assume—namely that economic growth is necessarily positive, instead pointing to the environmentally destructive, exploitative, and inequitable character of what is commonly considered economic progress.

The continuing skepticism about global free trade proposals shared by many environmental and consumer organizations—and their opposition to NAFTA—were based on more nuts-and-bolts considerations as well. These include the lack of funding and oversight to ensure that environmental regulations are enforced; the absence of public participation; the lack of rules governing production processes, sovereignty issues; and the lack of clear language defending the rights of communities and nations to set nondiscriminatory health, safety, and environmental regulations.

A common complaint among critics of NAFTA and GATT is that international trade regulations override democratic processes. Not only do the negotiations themselves take place behind closed doors with little opportunity for participation by citizens and non-governmental organizations, but the dispute process for settling conflicts between trading parties is completely closed to citizen involvement and review. According to the 1992 agreement, only the executive branch of each party was to be empowered to bring a complaint to the Free Trade Commission that NAFTA called for to resolve disputes. Individuals, unions, environmental groups, and local and state governments needed to persuade their country's executive branch to make their case for them under NAFTA's terms. All arguments and documents presented to the commission would remain secret until fifteen days after the commission made its decision, and if the parties agreed not to publish a final report of a given decision, the evidence and reasoning behind that decision would remain under wraps.[165]

Compounding the lack of citizen scrutiny and participation is the undue influence exercised by major corporate interests in the negotiating process. Not only are corporate representatives asked to participate in government working committees on international trade, but these same interests are also generally the ones who help write international standards for pesticide use, food safety, and consumer products.[166]

For both environmental and consumer groups, right-to-know provisions should also be incorporated into free trade agreements. International product-labeling requirements would give consumers information about the substances and technologies used in making imported goods, while workers would have access to similar information under right-to-know principles.

Closed dispute procedures, ambiguous language, and the lack of strong guarantees in NAFTA left open the possibility that environmental and consumer protection regulations would not be insulated from trade-motivated challenges. Environmental and consumer groups want better guarantees that local, state, and national standards will be respected. In this regard, they say that regulations that protect consumers and the environment should not be open to challenge simply because they are stricter than the international standard. Similarly, they argue that international standards should be considered mainly a regulation floor rather than a ceiling. Simply because a product is acceptable by the international standard does not mean that the affected government should not follow its own review and approval procedures for new products.

One of the key trade issues for environmentalists and consumer advocates is the need to apply standards to production processes as well as to products themselves. Such standards would protect the regional environment and cut down on destructive competition by ensuring that imports are not produced in a manner that would violate environmental or health laws in the importing country. NAFTA failed to distinguish itself from GATT in this regard, a fact that worries environmentalists. They looked, for example, for NAFTA expressly to reject GATT's interpretation of the rules regarding the tuna and dolphin dispute, thus making room for unilateral environmental measures that have an extraterritorial effect.

Environmentalists share labor activists' fear that even if free trade agreements protect local regulations, higher standards will be undermined as investment and jobs flow to countries with lower standards. Free trade agreements, they argue, must go further to facilitate the upward harmonization of health and environmental regulations to ensure that "pollution haven" investment does not result. In this regard, funding mechanisms are essential to guarantee that countries like Mexico have the capacity to enforce their environmental laws. Furthermore, they say that lack of enforcement of such laws should constitute an unfair trade practice.

The fear that U.S. investment will seek pollution havens in Mexico stems from the basic disparities in environmental laws and enforcement between the United States and Mexico. But free traders argue that more integrated regional and global markets will promote economic growth. With this growth will come expanded environmental consciousness among a growing Mexican middle class and increased revenues to support strong environmental programs. Most environmentalist organizations reject such reasoning, charging instead that economic growth inevitably means increased resource depletion and pollution without necessarily leading to tougher environmental regulation. In the best of circumstances, free trade without proper safeguards, funding, and guidelines may generate short-term economic gain for both trading partners but will not result in long-term or sustainable growth, according to environmental critics.[167]

Sovereignty, Internationalism, and Protectionism

Sovereignty and internationalism are two concepts that environmentalists and consumer advocates are struggling to reconcile. It is commonly agreed that the sovereign right of nations to protect their citizenry, conserve their environments, and uphold social values must be recognized in free trade agreements. But at the same time certain international rules and norms are clearly needed to protect the global environment and to regulate the increasingly global economy. To make such global standards meaningful, nations must cede some of their sovereignty.

Generally, the more industrialized nations would benefit from an upward harmonization of environmental and health standards. As all standards improved, less developed countries would be less able to use lower standards as a type of indirect subsidy to their exporting industries, and corporations from the more developed nations would have less incentive to relocate. But countries like Mexico could rightly charge that their sovereignty would be undermined if they were forced to abide by the regulations established by more developed and wealthier nations. Reacting to demands by environmentalists and consumer advocates for phased-in upward harmonization, a spokesperson for the Bush State Department accused U.S. environmentalists of being "latter-day colonialists" and said that such proposals were simply a "new justification for keeping the Latins down."[168]

Sovereignty also becomes an issue with recent proposals to regulate the foreign operations of U.S. corporations and to create increased access to foreign citizens with complaints against U.S. investors or products. One such proposal is for a U.S. Foreign Environmental Practices Act, modeled after the Foreign Corrupt Practices Act, which would make U.S. citizens and corporations subject to both criminal and civil prosecution in U.S. courts for violating applicable U.S. environmental law. Such a law would probably go a long way toward persuading U.S. corporations investing in Mexico to improve their environmental practices. Its supporters say that it would also increase corporate accountability by making firms more responsible to consumers, workers, and the communities in which they invest. Given the fact that Mexican courts will not consider suits against corporations for violating environmental laws, this proposal has gained support among many Mexican as well as U.S. environmentalists. But for other Mexicans such proposals revive fears of Yankee domination. Mexican problems should be resolved by Mexicans, they say.[169]

In relation to free trade, the sovereignty debate also extends to such issues as saving the family farm, protecting small businesses, restricting the exploitation of natural resources, and fostering certain industries as part of a national development policy. Questions of sovereignty also come into play when considering whether free trade agreements should contain clauses requiring respect for basic human, labor, and political rights.

If free trade is to be more than a corporate bill of rights, such issues need to be considered in establishing rules for global and regional integration. Strong and enforceable norms for basic human rights are essential to guarantee that countries do not achieve unfair trade advantages because their workers are repressed and exploited. Such standards already exist in the UN's International Labor Organization and in the UN's Universal Declaration of Human Rights.[170]

Linking free trade agreements to this kind of internationalism would help ensure a level playing field for trade. Arguments about national sovereignty represent the worst kind of protectionism when they defend a country's failure to meet international standards for human rights, labor organizing, and political freedom. But a new world order cannot and should not mean one in which communities and nations no longer have the right to protect their own social or cultural values or to set their own development policies.

The ideal of free trade and global integration must make room for such protections if economies are to grow and societies are to prosper. Even if some economic inefficiencies and trade barriers are involved, free trade agreements should allow for measures that save family farms, sustain local cultures, or protect other important social values of trade partners. Similarly, community and national economic development goals—such as food security, agrarian reform programs, or industrial development policies—

cannot be ignored simply to make it easier for transnational investors and traders to conduct their business.

Some of the harshest criticism of NAFTA and U.S. free trade initiatives has come from Ralph Nader's consumer watchdog group Public Citizen. Nader has accused GATT of "imposing a mega-corporate view of the world." Staff attorney Lori Wallach charged that the revisions reflected in the final NAFTA draft were merely cosmetic and that the two side agreements reached in 1993 did not do nearly enough to outweigh the overall negative impact of the proposed agreement. According to Wallach, "The United States and other nations are at a crossroads. The rapidly expanding global marketplace threatens to overwhelm citizens' ability to exercise democratic sovereignty by legislating rules that will govern their societies. Multinational corporations want global commerce but without corresponding global law to hold them accountable."[171]

Shaping the Alternatives

Free trade by itself will not solve Mexico's development problems, reinvigorate the U.S. economy, or make the Western Hemisphere more competitive in the global market. Developing needed infrastructure and paying social costs like educating the young, retraining displaced workers, preventing and remediating environmental degradation, and safeguarding the public health are tasks that can only be accomplished by managing the integration process to promote equity and sustainable development.

Neoliberal trade and investment agreements like NAFTA, however, rely on market forces to pay these costs. Deregulation, unfettered foreign investment, privatization, liberalized trade, and public sector austerity are supposed to lead to economic growth. The benefits of growth, in turn, are to trickle down to workers and other participants in the emerging economic order. But after a decade of liberalization and deregulation in the United States and Mexico, falling real incomes, sharply increased poverty rates, rising long-term unemployment, widening gaps between rich and poor, infrastructure decay, and environmental deterioration shot holes through these market-based approaches to development. Corporate and national competitive strategies based on low wages and feeble protections for workers eroded living standards and undermined unions and other representatives of working people. Of even greater concern, mechanisms like the accession clause to NAFTA, programs like the Enterprise for the Americas Initiative, and global frameworks like GATT threaten to spread these economic strategies and their deficiencies throughout the hemisphere and around the world.

Economic problems like these, with their potentially negative effects on political stability, are not the inevitable outcomes of increased trade and investment flows. Economic integration and expanding trade can be made to serve a broader agenda embracing social values. The goal is to construct a framework for integration that protects human beings, their communities, and the environment, not just the trade and investment decisions of transnational corporations. Constructing agreements that explicitly aim to defend labor rights and working conditions, build and rebuild livable communities, safeguard the environment, and protect the public health requires mechanisms that guide market forces to compensate for problems generated by unrestricted development.[172] These mechanisms fall into four related categories: democratization of the decisionmaking process, compensatory financing, legal and normative frameworks, and institutional innovations.

Out of the Back Rooms

Transparency, accountability, and public participation are prerequisites for a fully functioning economic and political system based on equity and sustainability. Because of the weighty decisions being made and their wide-ranging impacts, the process of integration and the formulation of agreements like NAFTA make it crucial that those who have traditionally been left out of the decision-making process advance their own agendas, projects, and alternatives in policy forums. "Perhaps the most important question dodged by NAFTA enthusiasts," noted a team of concerned observers, "is who should be making the vital decisions about the shape of the increasingly intertwined future of the three North American nations."[173] As traditionally structured, most of those decisions are made by free traders in government and corporate leaders with a vested interest in minimizing constraints on their international activities.

In addition to the negotiating process itself, international economic frameworks such as GATT and agreements like NAFTA undermine democracy by taking important decision-making powers out of the hands of local, state, and national elected leaders and vesting them in unelected, unrepresentative, and unaccountable institutions.[174] For example, the Free Trade Commission mandated by NAFTA and the two commissions set up under the parallel accords included only government officials, excluding independent representatives from sectors like labor, consumers, and community groups who would often be better able to evaluate the effects of policy on their constituents. Negotiations held in secret and disputes settled behind closed doors do little to ensure that the needs and concerns of affected communities and interest groups are taken into account, much less protected. By allowing international trade agreements to preempt local and national regulations in areas such as product safety, democracy is further weakened. In many cases these standards and regulations are the product of years of work by activists who used the legislatures and the courts to devise safeguards for the environment and for public health. Undermining their efforts not only does not advance democracy, it sets it back.

More is required than just pulling back the curtain on decision-making sessions held by others. Transparency and disclosure are not enough, although they are fundamental if affected members of the U.S. and Mexican publics are going to make informed choices about their options and strategies as integration progresses. From community right-to-know legislation to electoral reform and human rights protections, to representation on commissions with the power to oversee integration and implement policies, the democratization process must allow wide-ranging participation. As a consequence, democratic structures are a necessary component of all the other institutions and legal and normative frameworks that might complement trade and investment accords.

Compensatory Financing

Democratic openness and participation help equalize the political influence of government and business elites vis-à-vis other affected parties, such as labor, community groups, and environmentalists. But adjustments also have to be made for persistent North-South differences and for the economic disparities between those who are likely to benefit from integration and those who—at least in the short term—are likely to suffer. In addition, knotty problems such as transboundary pollution and resource depletion that are bound to be worsened by unrestrained development present funding dilemmas for both governments. Each of these difficulties raises obstacles to integration and diminishes its appeal to groups that are negatively affected, yet each can be ameliorated if solutions to them are pursued with the vigor that has been devoted to free trade.

Compensatory financing mechanisms are needed to help Mexico—the more disadvantaged economy—make the costly changes required by integration.[175] The costs of integrating Mexico's economy with regional and global markets will sharply expand the country's need for capital, both foreign and domestic. But the capital flows likely to enter the country during the years when most critical adjustments are being made are not likely to be enough to meet the need, especially given the global slowdown that has squeezed the international economy in recent years. Without some sort of compensatory mechanism, the Mexican government will be encouraged to solve its adjustment problems, reduce debt and unemployment, and resolve other economic issues by competing for capital based on low wages and lax regulations. To help avoid such strategies and to pay for aspects of integration like developing infrastructure and installing new norms and standards, compensatory financing is essential. As opposition leader Cuauhtémoc Cárdenas explained, "Making the fundamental disparity of the three economies the cornerstone of the [free trade] agreement means making compensatory financing its centerpiece."[176]

Mexico, however, will not be the only party that suffers at least temporary dislocation and increased financial pressures from integration. Workers in the United States and Canada who lose jobs to runaways, family farmers and the rural poor in all three countries, and communities buffeted by plant closures and other results of economic transformation will require assistance if sustainable and equitable integration is to go forward.

Providing financing for these and other needs might be the task of a new institution like the North American Development Bank and Adjustment Fund (NADBAF) proposed by three economists.[177] Capitalized by contributions from participating countries and modest taxes on international transactions, the bank could help protect communities, workers, and the environment. Modeled on initiatives like the European Regional Development Fund and the European Social Fund, created to facilitate integration of poorer members into the European Community, the bank could finance both long-term development projects and short-term adjustment strategies. Among the many possible uses of NADBAF financing are worker training and retraining, retooling and other conversion investments, job creation in rural areas, health and safety programs, and the development and upward harmonization of norms, standards, and regulations. Support for such projects is critical in order to keep a safety net under those at risk and to accelerate rises in wages, working conditions, and social standards in the North American economy as a whole.

Legal and Normative Frameworks

Another important way to help shape integration is to position trade and investment agreements within a larger structure of international legal and normative frameworks. These frameworks, like the United Nations conventions on civil, political, economic, and cultural rights, indicate priorities and aspirations and enforce pro-people and pro-environment provisions. There are many options for such frameworks, ranging from those with rather specific objectives—like devising a "code of conduct" for transnational corporations—to those with very broad-ranging agendas like a North American social and environmental charter.[178]

International frameworks like these help compensate for the declining ability of national governments and their citizens to oversee and restrain the international activities of TNCs and other transnational actors. They also bind the signatory governments themselves to pursue policies and paths of development consistent with the goals outlined in the agreements. If constructed with adequate enforcement mechanisms, such as an international court and trade sanctions, these international frameworks may provide avenues for nations, nongovernmental organizations, communities, and even individuals to pursue legal judgments outside domestic court systems when provisions of the agreements are violated. Finally, when devised so that trade and investment policies are linked to social issues, they can help make sure that the effects of one upon the other are considered in tandem and not artificially separated.

International agreements on labor, migration, and human rights, for instance, would be logical components of a broad package of initiatives designed to commit governments to protecting and upgrading living conditions in the hemisphere.[179] With economic integration will come increased social, cultural, and political integration, requiring commitments to manage the process and remedy ill effects. Trade and investment relations will spill over into these other areas by spurring at least temporary increases in migration, for example, or by threatening labor rights as governments and corporations pursue low-wage and union-repressive competitive strategies. From ratification of the American Convention for Human Rights to totally new agreements on issues like migration, these instruments would obligate the U.S. and Mexican governments to deal with these social by-products of integration. Specialized bodies that allow substantive access by all affected parties—a "North American Human Rights Commission" and a "North American Human Rights Court," for instance—could be given jurisdiction over disputes and litigation arising from the pacts.[180]

The most extensive proposal to come out of considerations like these has been for a social charter modeled on the one passed by the European Community as part of its own integration process.[181] A North American social and environmental charter, for example, would commit the signatory governments gradually to standardize norms relating to issues like labor rights, migration, and the environment. Linked to NAFTA or some similar trade agreement, the charter would be designed to ensure that the conditions under which people live and work in the North American countries would be harmonized in an upward direction and not allowed to fall as part of the bidding war for capital.

It is not that such a charter could overcome the vast gaps in living conditions that separate the United States or Canada from Mexico. Instead, by recognizing that people in each country have congruent and effective rights to collective bargaining, community right-to-know, occupational health and safety, and other such protections, the charter would provide a trilateral, enforceable set of "threshold protections" for workers, their communities, and the environment.[182] By including provisions for democratic participation and accountability in the institutions set up to enforce the charter, such a document would advance not only the economic and social rights of the region's citizens but their political rights and influence as well.

Institutional Innovations

Carrying out a successful, equitable, and sustainable form of economic integration requires representative and accountable institutions, many of which must be created anew. In addition to the institutions described above, bi- and trilateral commissions and similar bodies are needed to guide integration and manage its challenges. The number and mandates of these new institutions should be broad enough to encompass all aspects of integration and to account for the full social costs that will accompany the integration process. From health care and labor standards to housing, education, taxation, and debt, there are manifold tasks for such community-based institutions to accomplish.

Along the U.S.-Mexico border, for example, a binational commission with fund-raising and enforcement authority could monitor and find solutions to health, environmental, and labor problems.[183] In a similar vein, a Sustainable Development Commission composed of representatives from public interest, business, and governmental organizations could assess and, if necessary, overrule provisions of trade accords like NAFTA or attempts to implement them because of their impacts on the environment.[184] Commissions for labor and social welfare, international work councils linking unionists employed by the same transnational employers, and a commission on political democracy could also be established to advance people-based agendas and direct investments to meeting social needs.

The proceedings of these institutions should be public, and documents, decisions, hearing dates, and the like will need to be readily available to all interested parties in order to achieve the goal of transparency. In addition, in most cases at least, participants and decision makers who sit on the bodies should be elected, not appointed. If they are appointed, the process must be carefully structured in order to maximize public input. For instance, participants might be chosen from a slate of candidates nominated by organizations that are recognized leaders among such sectors as labor, environmentalists, community activists, health care providers, business associations, and consumer groups. To preserve accountability, some community recall provision must also be included so that participants on these bodies can be removed if their constituents do not think that their interests are being served. To guarantee independence, the institutions must have fund-raising mechanisms built into their structures, whether derived from user fees, taxation, or dedicated funding from government or community funds.

Uphill Battle

Creating a welter of new institutions, laws, regulations, and bureaucracies is not the objective of these suggested strategies. Shaping the emerging economic order in a way that preserves a livable and fruitful environment for future generations and provides healthy, safe, and satisfying living conditions for the hemisphere's people are the goals of such endeavors. In order to accomplish these difficult but reasonable objectives, the policy-making terrain must be reclaimed from those who are shielded from the fallout of their decisions inside the bunker of ideology, wealth, and power. Because of the way NAFTA was structured by the Bush and Salinas administrations, however, enhancing citizen participation in the decision-making process is an uphill battle. This structure was not altered by the parallel agreements tacked on by the Clinton administration.

As negotiated, NAFTA offered few options for challenge by communities or interest groups. The dispute resolution mechanism, for instance, was so secret that relevant documents were not to be available to interested parties who were not directly involved in the dispute. Nor were members of the public—environmentalists, labor, and consumer groups, for example—to be eligible to bring cases up for resolution or to be present at hearings. Because NAFTA was not submitted to the U.S. Congress as a treaty, it was open to court challenges when and if it preempted local standards. As a last resort, opponents can push their legislatures to abrogate the pact if it is approved, but that would likely be a lengthy process during which time potentially damaging structural changes in the economies of the United States and Mexico would go forward.

As a consequence of this grim forecast, when NAFTA was signed by Bush and Salinas in late 1992, those who sought trade-linked protections for labor, consumers, and the environment redoubled their efforts either to kill the trade pact or to get it renegotiated. The 1992 national elections in the United States boosted their chances slightly. Not only was the neoliberal government of George Bush removed from office, but an exceptionally large number of new representatives were elected to Congress, most on platforms calling for an end to business as usual in Washington.

President Clinton attempted to juggle competing constituencies—corporations, organized labor, environmentalists, ethnic minorities, and the poor—by endorsing NAFTA on the condition that parallel agreements with Canada and Mexico, along with domestic legislation, protect the environment and the rights of workers. But the two additional agreements reached by the NAFTA partners in 1993 satisfied few of the pact's critics and left the Democratic Party badly split on the issue.

Whatever the outcome of the battle over NAFTA, however, the fair trade campaign offered a crucial opportunity to begin building international coalitions and generating a broad-based vision of democracy and economic development. Sustained efforts on both of these fronts are essential if the profit-driven corporate agenda for economic integration is to be replaced by a citizens agenda incorporating such broader values as equity, democracy, diversity, and sustainability.

References

1. The description of this process comes from interviews with Shigemasa Ito and Gilberto Ibarra, executives of Hitachi Consumer Products de México, S.A. de C.V.

2. The "industrializing" South refers largely to middle-income countries, including most of Latin America. Few of the world's poorest nations will find that Mexico's strategy is relevant to them.

3. *Economic Adjustment and Worker Dislocation in a Competitive Society: Report of the Secretary of Labor's Task Force on Economic Adjustment and Worker Dislocation* (Washington, DC: U.S. Department of Labor, Dec. 1986) and U.S. Congress, Office of Technology Assessment, *Technology and Structural Unemployment: Reemploying Displaced Adults*, OTA-ITE-250 (Washington, DC, Feb. 1986). The Bureau of Labor Statistics defines "displaced" workers as those who permanently lost their jobs after at least three years in their positions.

4. Lisa Oppenheim, "Introduction," *Labor Research Review* 19 (Chicago: Midwest Center for Labor Research, 1992).

5. Comprehensive descriptions of the changing U.S. economy can be found in Donald Barlett and James Steele, *America: What Went Wrong?* (Kansas City, MO: Andrews and McMeel, 1992); Bennett Harrison and Barry Bluestone, *The Great U-Turn: Corporate Restructuring and the Polarizing of America* (New York: Basic Books, 1988); and Juliet Schor, *The Overworked American: The Unexpected Decline of Leisure* (New York: Basic Books, 1991). See also the Economic Policy Institute's voluminous collection of employment and wage data for the decade in Lawrence Mishel and Jared Bernstein, *Declining Wages for High School and College Graduates: Pay and Benefits Trends by Education, Gender, Occupation, and State, 1979-1991* (Washington, DC: Economic Policy Institute, 1992).

6. The accumulated value of foreign direct investment in the United States rose from $83 billion in 1980 to $403 billion in 1990 (measured in current dollars). *Survey of Current Business* (Washington, DC: U.S. Department of Commerce, Aug. 1991). See also Norman J. Glickman and Douglas P. Woodward, *The New Competitors: How Foreign Investors Are Changing the U.S. Economy* (New York: Basic Books, 1989).

7. Leading advocates of neoliberal policy during the 1980s were Treasury Secretary Donald Regan and Office of Management and Budget directors David Stockman and Richard Darman. An important think tank supporting continued efforts to use GATT to open international trade is the Institute for International Economics in Washington, DC. See, for example, William Cline, ed., *Trade Policy in the 1980s* (Washington, DC: Institute for International Economics, 1983).

8. One of the most visible proponents of the *realeconomik* strategy is Clyde V. Prestowitz, a former U.S. trade negotiator. See his book *Trading Places: How We Allowed Japan to Take the Lead* (New York: Basic Books, 1988).

9. One prominent industrial policy advocate argues that it is not the competitive position of U.S.-*based* corporations that matters, but rather the competitiveness of corpora-

tions *operating* in the United States, whether foreign- or domestic-owned. Even more important, he argues, are the specific functions that corporations decide to locate in the country—engineering or assembly, for example. See Robert Reich, *The Work of Nations: Preparing Ourselves for 21st-Century Capitalism* (New York: Alfred A. Knopf, 1991).

10. For a discussion of the addition of a regional strategy to the United States' traditional multilateral approach, see Sidney Weintraub, "Regionalism and the GATT: The North American Initiative," *SAIS Review* (Winter-Spring 1991). Note that in addition to the trade-related reasons discussed here, the Bush administration was motivated by a desire to support Salinas politically and to reward his economic reforms.

11. According to Treasury Secretary James Baker, the Canada-U.S. Free Trade Agreement "is also a lever to achieve more open trade. Other nations are forced to recognize that the United States will devise ways to expand trade—with or without them. If they choose not to open markets, they will not reap the benefits." *The International Economy* (Jan.-Feb. 1988), 41, cited in Peter Morici, *Trade Talks with Mexico: A Time for Realism* (Washington, DC: National Planning Association, 1991), 113. Note that this lever will only work when other national leaders share the neoliberal perspective.

12. Clinton detailed his position on trade policy in a speech at North Carolina State University on 4 Oct. 1992. "Without a national economic strategy," he said, "this country has been allowed to drift. Meanwhile, our competitors have organized themselves around clear national goals to save, promote, and enhance high-wage, high-growth jobs. . . . We have to have an overall trade policy that says to our trading partners, particularly our wealthy ones, if you want access to our market, you've got to give us access to yours."

13. Two valuable studies of development in South Korea, Taiwan, and Singapore are Walden Bello and Stephanie Rosenfeld, *Dragons in Distress: Asia's Miracle Economies in Crisis* (San Francisco: Institute for Food and Development Policy, 1990), and Frederic C. Deyo, ed., *The Political Economy of the New Asian Industrialism* (Ithaca, NY: Cornell University Press, 1987).

14. The failure of the Latin American NICs to turn investment into broad-based development was not due to a lack of foreign investment: Multinational corporations produced between 31 percent and 44 percent of these countries' industrial output, compared with 16 percent in Taiwan and 19 percent in South Korea. See Rhys Jenkins, "Learning from the Gang: Are There Lessons for Latin America from East Asia?" *Bulletin of Latin American Research* 10, no. 1 (1991).

15. An outstanding survey of dependency theory and an application of one version to Mexico is Gary Gereffi and Peter Evans, "Transnational Corporations, Dependent Development, and State Policy in the Semiperiphery: A Comparison of Brazil and Mexico," *Latin American Research Review* 16, no. 3 (1981). For a review of dependency theory in the light of evidence that third world governments can promote development, see Peter Evans, "After Dependency: Recent Studies of Class, State, and Industrialization," *Latin American Research Review* 20, no. 2 (1985).

16. Although ISI was already under way in practice in the 1930s, its theoretical underpinnings developed in the immediate post-World War II period. Leading the work was Raúl Prébisch, the first head of the United Nations' Economic Commission for Latin America and the Caribbean. For an examination of how ISI worked in Mexico, see James Cypher, *State and Capital in Mexico: Development Policy Since 1940* (Boulder, CO: Westview Press, 1990).

17. Mexico's petroleum industry, the second largest in the world after that of the United States, was almost entirely owned by seventeen British and U.S. firms. Agribusinesses in the United States owned millions of acres of rich land that they used to grow export crops such as cotton and sugar. One-quarter of Mexico's entire territory was in foreign hands by 1910. Foreign capitalists dominated the railroads, the mining industry, and

the banking sector. The United States was the largest source of foreign investment, with almost 40 percent of the total.

The role of foreign investment in Mexico during the *porfiriato* is described in Harry K. Wright, *Foreign Enterprise in Mexico: Laws and Policies* (Chapel Hill, NC: University of North Carolina Press, 1971); Roger D. Hansen, *The Politics of Mexican Development* (Baltimore: Johns Hopkins University Press, 1971); Mira Wilkins, *The Emergence of Multinational Enterprise: American Business Abroad from the Colonial Era to 1914* (Cambridge, MA: Harvard University Press, 1970); and Clark A. Reynolds, *The Mexican Economy: Twentieth-Century Structure and Growth* (New Haven, CT: Yale University Press, 1970).

18. By far the two most important oil companies were Standard Oil of New Jersey and Royal Dutch Shell, which together controlled more than 70 percent of total Mexican production in 1938. An exhaustive account of the oil expropriation is contained in Lorenzo Meyer, *Mexico and the United States in the Oil Controversy, 1917-1942* (Austin: University of Texas Press, 1977).

19. In nondurable consumer goods, imports fell from 22 percent of total demand in 1939 to 5 percent in 1969; in intermediate goods the decline was from 56 percent to 22 percent over the same period, and in capital and durable consumer goods the figure dropped from 91 percent to 51 percent, respectively. René Villarreal, *El desequilibrio externo, en la industrialización de México, 1929-1975* (Mexico, D.F.: FCE, 1979).

20. The decision not to challenge the rules of the international financial system was consistent with Mexico's conservative financial policies from the 1940s on. See Sylvia Maxfield, *Governing Capital: International Finance and Mexican Politics* (Ithaca, NY: Cornell University Press, 1990), and Judith A. Teichman, *Policy making in Mexico: From Boom to Crisis* (Boulder, CO: Westview Press, 1988).

21. One analysis of Mexico's shift to the position of "model debtor" is found in George Grayson, *Oil and Mexican Foreign Policy* (Pittsburgh: University of Pittsburgh Press, 1988), 47-51.

22. David Barkin, from the introduction to the Japanese edition of *Distorted Development* (Albuquerque: Latin American Data Base, 12 and 19 Aug. 1992).

23. Between 1984 and 1989 the proportion of national income received by the poorest tenth of Mexicans declined by 8.8 percent to roughly 1 percent of total national income. In the same period the wealthiest 10 percent increased its share of national income by 16 percent. Enrique Quintana, "Hombre rico, hombre pobre," *El Financiero*, 28 May 1992. In 1990 the government reported that forty-one million Mexicans fell below the poverty line, with seventeen million living in conditions of extreme poverty. Consejo Consultivo del Pronasol, "El combate a la pobreza: Lineamientos programáticos," cited in *La Jornada*, 1 Sept. 1990.

24. Gustavo Lomelin, "Reprivatization of Mexican Banks: A 'Sweet Deal' Expected to Consolidate and Enhance Inequality" (Albuquerque: Latin American Data Base, 1 May 1991). See also William Schomberg and Ted Bardacke, "Doing Business with the Big Boys," *El Financiero International*, 19 Oct. 1992, 14; Noe Cruz Serrano, "Privatization Enhances Monopoly and Oligopoly in Mexican Market" (Albuquerque: Latin American Data Base, 15 May 1991); and Noe Cruz Serrano, "Tan sólo 5 emporios compraron 30 paraestatales de 148 vendidas," *El Financiero*, 19 June 1990.

25. For a discussion of the varied extent to which Latin American governments are shifting economic decision-making power to the private sector, see "Latin America in the 1980s," *International Economic Insight* (Nov.-Dec. 1990).

26. *Economic and Social Progress in Latin America: 1992 Report*, Table B-2 (Washington, DC: Inter-American Development Bank, 1992), and "Two Private Studies Say Government's Targeted Three Percent G.D.P. Growth Rate for 1993 Is Unrealistic" (Albuquerque: Latin American Database, 10 Feb. 1993). Several estimates made in mid-1993

estimated per capita GDP growth rates between -0.1 percent and 0.4 percent for that year.

27. Agency for International Development, *U.S. Overseas Loans and Grants and Assistance from International Organizations* (Washington, DC, n.d.), and the U.S. Council of the Mexico-U.S. Business Committee, "Report on Mexico: Recent Economic Developments," 2nd q., 19 June 1992. For a brief description of the cozy relationship between the World Bank and Mexican economic planners, see Damian Fraser, "Like Minds Underpin Mexico-Bank Intimacy," *Financial Times*, 3 March 1992.

28. American Chamber of Commerce in Mexico, "The Role of Development Banks in U.S.-Mexico Trade," *Review of Trade and Industry*, 2nd q., 1992.

29. In 1983 total binational trade stood at $25.9 billion, rising to an estimated $71 billion in 1992. "Total trade" means both U.S. exports to and imports from Mexico. These figures include the full value of maquiladora trade and are not adjusted for inflation. M. Angeles Villarreal, "Mexico-U.S. Merchandise Trade," *CRS Report for Congress* (Washington, DC: Congressional Research Service, 26 Aug. 1992). The most readily available and oft-cited data for foreign direct investment (FDI) in Mexico is compiled by two agencies within Mexico's Ministry of Trade and Industrial Development (SE-COFI). These data record not the actual investment amounts but the amount that a firm has requested permission to invest. These figures therefore probably overstate the actual levels of FDI since firms are likely to request amounts greater than they expect to invest to avoid going through the investment approval process again in case of a cost overrun. In addition, investment financed through domestic borrowing is counted by SECOFI as FDI, but it does not represent actual inflows of foreign exchange.

30. Data from Villarreal, "Mexico-U.S. Merchandise Trade" (ibid.). At $4.3 billion in 1991, oil represents over 15 percent of U.S. imports from Mexico. Over half of Mexico's petroleum exports go to the United States. In 1990 Mexico was the third most important supplier of oil to the U.S. market behind Saudi Arabia and Nigeria. Mexico is the third largest export market (after the former Soviet Union and Japan) for U.S. agricultural commodities, and it is the second largest supplier of U.S. agricultural imports. The leading U.S. agricultural exports to Mexico are corn, sorghum, soybeans, dairy products, seeds, and animal fats, while the United States imports tropical products and specialty crops, including coffee, vegetables, fruits and nuts, and cattle.

31. In 1990 Mexican direct foreign investment in the United States was $554 million out of nearly $404 billion in total direct foreign investment. *Survey of Current Business* (Washington, DC: U.S. Department of Commerce, Aug. 1991).

32. See Andrew J. Samet and Gary C. Hufbauer, *"Unfair" Trade Practices: A Mexican-American Drama*, U.S.-Mexico Project Series Working Paper No. 1 (Washington, DC: Overseas Development Council, 1982), and Steven E. Sanderson, *The Transformation of Mexican Agriculture: International Structure and the Politics of Rural Change* (Princeton, NJ: Princeton University Press, 1986), especially Chapter Two.

33. *Access Mexico* (Arlington, VA: Cambridge Data and Development, 1992).

34. *Mexico: Country Profile 1991-92* (London: Economist Intelligence Unit, 1992). In 1992, consumer imports represented 17.4 percent of total imports, intermediate goods 57.6 percent, and capital goods 25 percent. "Business Indicators," *Business Mexico*, July 1993, 54. Including maquiladora trade alters the proportions for 1992 to 12 percent, 69 percent, and 19 percent, respectively. *Country Report Mexico* (London: Economist Intelligence Unit, June 8, 1993), 4.

35. From a report on the program in *La Jornada*, 1 Oct. 1992, 28, cited in David Barkin, "The New Shape of the Countryside: Agrarian Counterreform in Mexico," carried on PeaceNet (San Francisco: Institute for Global Communications, 22 Nov. 1992).

36. Tim Golden, "The Dream of Land Dies Hard in Mexico," *New York Times*, 27 Nov. 1991, A1.

37. SECOFI, "La inversión extranjera en Mexico," *Comercio Exterior* 3, no. 3 (March 1993):213.

38. These agricultural trade data come largely from "Agricultural Trade—Big Business for U.S. and Mexico," *Agricultural Outlook* (March 1992), and "U.S.-Mexico Agricultural Trade under a NAFTA," *Agricultural Outlook* (June 1992). The figure for broccoli is from Western Growers Association, "The Effects on the U.S. Agricultural Sector of a Free Trade Agreement with Mexico," in a hearing before the U.S. House of Representatives Committee on Agriculture, *Proposed United States-Mexico Free-Trade Agreement and Fast-track Authority*, 102nd Cong., 1st sess., 24 April 1991, 323.

39. SECOFI, "La inversión extranjera" (see n. 37).

40. Rosa Elena Montes de Oca, "Las empresas trasnacionales en la industria alimentaria mexicana," in Rodolfo Echeverría Zuno, ed., *Transnacionales, agricultura y alimentación* (Mexico, D.F.: Colegio Nacional de Economistas and Editorial Nueva Imagen, 1982).

41. The top seven firms in terms of Mexican debt and capital offerings abroad were based in the United States, as were eight of the top ten. Rossana Fuentes Berain and Ignacio Rodríguez, "Brokers Prosper in Mexican Miracle," *El Financiero International*, 20 April 1992.

42. SECOFI, "La inversión extranjera" (see n. 37).

43. SECOFI, "La inversión extranjera" (see n. 37). The Mexican government considers foreign investment in the stock market to be foreign direct investment, but by most definitions "direct investment" and "portfolio investment" (meaning the purchase of stocks, bonds, and other securities) are distinct items. According to Mexican law, the stock shares owned by foreigners are nonvoting, meaning that they carry no managerial control but do represent a claim on assets and are entitled to the same dividends as Mexican-owned shares.

44. Foreign investment in the stock market dropped by 28.53 percent, from $27 billion on 31 May to $19.4 billion on 24 July. Much of this is due to the declining value of shares, but foreign investors withdrew $5.339 billion (U.S.) from the stock market between May and Aug. 1992, according to the central bank and the *Bolsa. SourceMex* (Albuquerque: Latin American Data Base, 6 Aug. 1992 and 23 Sept. 1992). Also see Matt Moffett, "Mexican Market Sees Foreigners Streaming Out," *Wall Street Journal*, 18 June 1992, C1, and "Pressure for Devaluation Builds," *The Mexico Report* (7 July 1992), 1. Analysts blamed the exodus on a number of factors, including possible presidential candidate Ross Perot's statements opposing a free trade agreement. That such external politicking should have so great an impact on the Mexican market worried observers, prompting some to call for greater government regulation.

45. "Mexico Is Easing Rules on Making Petrochemicals," *Wall Street Journal*, 18 Aug. 1992. The government maintains exclusive control of the production of ethanol, propane, butanes, pentanes, hexane, heptane, and raw materials used in processing selected oils and lubricants, according to a *Notimex* news service report on 18 Aug. 1992 (Albuquerque: Latin American Data Base).

46. A further regulatory change allowed up to 100 percent foreign ownership of secondary petrochemicals through the use of a trust fund held by a Mexican bank.

47. Maquiladoras in the textile industry must be 51 percent Mexican-owned. The textile industry is subject to export quotas under the Multilateral Fibre Agreement, to which both the United States and Mexico are parties.

48. Despite the constitutional prohibition against foreign ownership of any land within 62.5 miles (a hundred kilometers) of the border, foreign businesses gain the ownership rights they want through *fideicomisos*, which are thirty-year trusts that make

Mexican banks the legal owner of land but grant foreign businesses primary use of the property. If a new foreign investment law President Salinas planned to submit to Congress in 1993 passes, any company incorporated in Mexico reportedly will be able to purchase land in Mexico's forbidden border zone. If true, maquilas would no longer need *fideicomisos*.

49. Quoted in *Business Mexico*, Feb. 1986.

50. A vast literature exists on the maquiladoras. Probably the best source of data, analysis, and historic detail is Leslie Sklair, *Assembling for Development: The Maquila Industry in Mexico and the United States* (Winchester, MA: Unwin Hyman, 1989). Other valuable sources include Joseph Grunwald and Kenneth Flamm, eds., *The Global Factory: Foreign Assembly in International Trade* (Washington, DC: Brookings, 1985), and *The Use and Economic Impact of TSUS Items 806.30 and 807.00* (Washington, DC: U.S. International Trade Commission, 1988).

51. Of the 2,042 maquiladoras operating in June 1992, 12 percent were located outside the six Mexican border states and another 9 percent were located more than 12.5 miles (20 kilometers) from the border within the border states. American Chamber of Commerce, *Maquiladora Newsletter*, third quarter (1992). According to Sklair, the main differences between border and nonborder maquilas are the latter's lower wages, inferior infrastructure, and the greater propensity to purchase local supplies. Sklair, *Assembling for Development* (ibid.).

52. Data from Mexico's National Institute of Statistics, Geography, and Information (INEGI) and the Ministry of Programming and Budget (SPP), cited in Business International Corp., *Succeeding in the New Mexico: Corporate Strategy, Globalization and the Free Trade Agreement* (New York, 1991), 198. Making the increase in value added per employee even more impressive is the fact that real wages were lower in 1989 than in 1983. The wage rate is relevant because wages make up a large portion of value added in the maquiladoras.

53. Francisco Lara Valencia, "La fuerza de trabajo en la industria maquiladora de la región fronteriza de Sonora: Caracteristicas socioeconomicas y transición ocupacional," paper prepared for the XV Simposio de Historia y Antropología de Sonora, Hermosillo, Sonora, 21-24 Feb. 1990, 6.

54. Data from SECOFI cited in *La Jornada*, 14 Dec. 1992.

55. Fixed direct investment in the maquiladoras has been estimated at $5 billion. Leslie Sklair, *The Maquiladoras: Present Status, Future Potential*, study submitted to the U.S. Office of Technology Assessment (Dec. 1991). This amount implies average annual investment of more than $600 million assuming standard depreciation rates. It is impossible to know how much of the direct investment is recorded in Mexico since a great deal of the equipment used in maquilas is leased from U.S.-based parent companies. In such cases the investment dollars stay in the United States.

56. See, for example, Roberto A. Sánchez, "Condiciones de vida de los trabajadores de la maquiladora en Tijuana y Nogales," *Frontera Norte* 4, no. 2 (July-Dec. 1990). The average total compensation cost per worker-hour in Mexican manufacturing as a whole was $2.17 in 1991. For the maquiladora sector by itself the figure was $1.55. These amounts reflect direct wages, benefits such as annual bonuses, vacations, and subsidized meals, and payroll taxes. From "International Comparisons of Hourly Compensation Costs for Production Workers in Manufacturing, 1991," Report 825 (Washington, DC: U.S. Department of Labor, Bureau of Labor Statistics, June 1992), and from unpublished data compiled by the Bureau of Labor Statistics.

57. Patricia A. Wilson, "The New Maquiladoras: Flexible Production in Low Wage Regions," in Khostrow Fatemi, ed., *Maquiladoras: Economic Problem or Solution?* (New York: Praeger, 1990). For the increasing productivity of maquila workers see Bernardo González-Aréchiga and José Carlos Ramiréz, "Productividad sin distribución: Cambio tec-

nológico en la industria maquiladora mexicana (1980-86)," *Frontera Norte* 1, no. 1 (Jan.-June 1989).

58. Harley Shaiken, "Myths about Mexican Workers," *DSC Report Series* (Washington, DC: Democratic Study Center, 29 June 1993).

59. *Twin Plant News*, Jan. 1987.

60. See, for example, U.S. Congress, Office of Technology Assessment, *U.S.-Mexico Trade: Pulling Together or Pulling Apart?* ITE-545 (Washington, DC: Government Printing Office, Oct. 1992), 81; G.W. Lucker, "The Hidden Costs of Worker Turnover: A Case Study in the Maquiladora Industry," *Journal of Borderlands Studies* 2 (1987); and Sklair, *Assembling for Development*, 179 (see n. 50).

61. Quoted in Harley Shaiken, "The Auto and Electronics Sectors in U.S.-Mexico Trade and Investment," study submitted to the U.S. Office of Technology Assessment (May 1992), 44-45.

62. Beginning in the late 1980s some researchers argued that the composition of maquiladoras was shifting toward increasingly high-technology industries and that maquiladoras were adopting new forms of work organization and greater training. See Jorge Carrillo, "Transformaciones en la industria maquiladora de exportación," in Bernardo González-Aréchiga and Rocío Barajas Escamilla, eds., *Las maquiladoras: Ajuste estructural y desarrollo regional* (Tijuana: COLEF and Fundación Friedrich Ebert, 1989), and Leonard Mertens and Laura Palomares, "El surgimiento de un nuevo tipo de trabajador en la industria de alta tecnología: El caso electrónico," in Estela Gutiérrez, ed., *Testimonios de la crisis I* (Mexico, D.F.: Siglo XXI, 1988).

  Many of these studies confused high-technology sectors, like electronics, with high-technology production processes. Furthermore, even where high-technology production processes were used, training requirements for line workers were still minimal, with training focused on plant technicians. One report that asserts that "training occupies a central place within the managerial strategies in the maquiladora plants" found nevertheless that only 25 percent of the plants surveyed offered technical training programs in the three years prior to the study. Jorge Carrillo, *Mercados de trabajo en la industria maquiladora de exportación* (Mexico: COLEF and STPS, 1991). For further exploration of these issues, see Wilson, "The New Maquiladoras" (n. 57); Harley Shaiken and Harry Browne, "Japanese Work Organization in Mexico," in Gabriel Székely, ed., *Manufacturing Across Borders and Oceans: Japan, the United States, and Mexico* (San Diego: Center for U.S.-Mexican Studies, 1991); and Cathryn L. Thorup, ed., *The United States and Mexico: Face to Face with New Technology* (New Brunswick, ME: Transaction Books, 1987).

63. Many maquiladoras dispense with the legal requirement for severance pay by renewing "temporary" twenty-eight-day work contracts until a worker is no longer needed. Since these temporary workers do not build up seniority, they can be dismissed at little cost.

64. U.S. Congress, Office of Technology Assessment, *U.S.-Mexico Trade*, 84 (see n. 60).

65. See Andrew Paxman, "Mexican Workers Give Trade Pact Mixed Review," *Christian Science Monitor*, 14 Aug. 1992.

66. There are many factors explaining this low level of domestic supply, including the failure of the government to mandate a local supply percentage, the low quality and inefficiency of many Mexican producers, and the unwillingness of Mexican industries to retool to meet the needs of firms that may withdraw their investment at any time. On the border, isolation from the Mexican interior and close commercial relations with the U.S. side (including a history of free trade) have discouraged the development of local industry.

67. Joseph Grunwald, "Opportunity Missed: Mexico and Maquiladoras," *Brookings Review* (Winter 1990-91).

68. For more on the "triple alliance," see Leslie Sklair, "The Maquila Industry and the Creation of a Transnational Capitalist Class in the United States-Mexico Border Region," in Lawrence A. Herzog, *Changing Boundaries in the Americas: New Perspectives on the U.S.-Mexican, Central American, and South American Borders* (San Diego: Center for U.S.-Mexican Studies, 1992), 69-88.

69. What little serious labor organizing there is in the maquilas has occurred in the Rio Grande Valley, mainly in Matamoros. See Edward J. Williams, "Attitudes and Strategies Inhibiting the Unionization of the Maquiladora Industry: Government, Industry, Unions, and Workers," *Journal of Borderland Studies* 6, no. 2, and Edward J. Williams and John T. Passé-Smith, *The Unionization of the Maquiladora Industry: The Tamaulipan Case in National Context* (San Diego: Institute for Regional Studies of the Californias, San Diego State University, 1992).

70. Peter Baird and Ed McCaughn, "Hit and Run: U.S. Runaway Shops on the Mexican Border," *Report on the Americas* (July-Aug. 1975).

71. Talli Nauman, "Maquiladoras Thrive Despite Doubts," *El Financiero International*, 9 Nov. 1992, and Brad Stratton, "Learning English Is Not Enough," *Quality Progress*, Jan. 1989.

72. In 1988, 44 percent of the maquilas and 75 percent of the jobs were found in specialized industrial parks for the maquila sector. Thomas P. Lee, ed., *In-Bond Industry/Industria Maquiladora* (Mexico, D.F.: Administración y Servicios Internacionales, 1988).

73. Mexican capitalists and professionals also play an important rôle in the maquila sector mainly by setting up industrial parks, providing services, and acting as subcontractors. See Alejandra Salas-Porras, "Maquiladoras y burguesía regional," *El Cotidiano*, Edición Especial, 1987.

74. Sklair, *Assembling for Development*, 235 (see n. 50).

75. The Programa Nacional Fronterizo (PRONAF) was established by President López Mateos in 1961 to promote social and economic development and make the border a "window on Mexico." The program was short-lived and not well-funded but it did result in the construction of the PRONAF tourist centers in Juárez and Tijuana.

76. This point is made well by Sklair, who observes, "The great hopes on which the maquila strategy rests, namely that Mexico could supply substantial quantities of material inputs to the maquila industry, backward linkages, and that it could derive massive, virtually free technology spinoffs and genuine technology transfers, have not been realized." This was based on a faulty understanding of the ideology and practice of production sharing, according to Sklair, *Assembling for Development*, 227 (see n. 50). Also see Joseph Grunwald, "U.S.-Mexican Production Sharing in World Perspective," in Paul Ganster, ed., *The Maquiladora Program in Trinational Perspective: Mexico, Japan, and the United States* (San Diego: Institute for Regional Studies of the Californias, San Diego State University, 1987).

77. For analysis of why Mexico has failed to increase domestic linkages and use the maquila sector to spur broader industrialization, see Patricia A. Wilson, "The Global Assembly Industry: Maquiladoras in International Perspective," Community and Regional Working Paper Series, no. 10 (Austin: University of Texas, July 1989), and Grunwald, "Opportunity Missed" (see n. 67).

78. Among such companies are Ansell International of Columbus, Ohio, a surgical glove manufacturer, and two producers of electronic components, Pulse Engineering and Valor Electronics.

79. In an imaginative effort to drive this point home, U.S. Representative James A. Traficant, Jr. (D-Ohio), introduced a bill in 1992 that would improve the competitive position of Ohio businesses by exempting them from otherwise applicable health, safety and wage standards.

80. Although this statistical treatment is logical, neither the United States nor multilateral institutions such as the International Monetary Fund, GATT, OECD, and the World Bank use this method. For the sake of consistency the trade figures used in this book include the value of in-bond imports and exports unless otherwise noted. In 1993 the Mexican central bank began to include maquila imports and exports in its merchandise trade figures, implicitly moving maquila wages from the services account to the goods account. At the time of publication it was not clear whether this change would be made permanent.

81. U.S. duty benefits extend beyond the re-import of U.S. components in some cases. By warehousing the maquila-assembled goods in U.S.-designated free-trade zones (FTZs) the importer can delay paying duties until the goods are sold or processed further. "In the case of the major automobile manufacturers with maquiladoras, the warehouses and transfer points in the border cities and the assembly plants in other regions of the United States, such as the upper Midwest, all are designated as FTZs. Consequently, the duties on the maquiladora products do not become due until the automobile is shipped from the plant to a dealer." James E. Groff and John P. McCray, "Maquiladoras: The Mexico Option Can Reduce Your Manufacturing Cost," *Management Accounting*, Jan. 1991.

82. Cited in José A. Méndez, Tracy Murray, and Donald J. Rousslang, "U.S.-Mexico Employment Effects of Repealing the U.S. Offshore Assembly Provision," *Applied Economics* 23 (1991):553-66.

83. Customs officials record OAP-qualified imports in two tariff lines now called HTS 9802.00.60 and 9802.00.80. These lines correspond to the pre-1990 tariff lines called TSUS 806.30 and 807.00. The total value of U.S. imports from Mexico under 806.30 and 807.00 in 1968 was $73 million. Since the proportion of nondutiable U.S.-made components and materials in maquila exports to the United States has held fairly constant at just over 50 percent over the years, the authors have estimated roughly $40 million in duty-free exports in 1968. See Sklair, *Assembling for Development*, 12 (see n. 50).

84. Note that Mexico's portion of the duty-free total of imports under TSUS 806.30 and 807.00 varies greatly from its portion of total imports under these codes. This is because Mexican maquiladoras use a much higher proportion of U.S.-made components in their assembly processes than do assemblers in developed countries such as Japan. As an illustration, in 1986 Mexico accounted for 18 percent of total imports under the Offshore Assembly Provision, but 54 percent of the duty-free portion of these imports.

85. A recent attempt to provide what Méndez et al. call "reasonable upper-bound estimates" for the employment effects of the tariff breaks led to the conclusion that repealing the Offshore Assembly Provision would have small, negative effects in both Mexico and the United States. See Méndez et al., "U.S.-Mexico Employment Effects" (n. 82). For a survey of several earlier estimations, see Gregory Schoepfle and Jorge Perez-Lopez, *U.S. Employment Impact of TSUS 806.30 and 807.00 Provisions and Mexican Maquiladoras: A Survey of Issues and Estimates*, Economic Discussion Paper 29, (Washington, DC: U.S. Department of Labor, Bureau of International Labor Affairs, 1988).

86. From 1980 to 1993, 144 companies moved 97,000 jobs from 253 U.S. work sites to their own subsidiaries in Mexico. Given the difficulties involved in tracking down all such runaways, the real numbers are probably much higher: The total jobs lost, for example, is probably close to 175,000. Harry Browne and Beth Sims, *Runaway America: U.S. Jobs and Factories on the Move* (Albuquerque: Resource Center Press, 1993).

87. One of the first of these was Form-O-Uth, which manufactured brassieres for Sears in California and Texas. The company closed its California plant in 1969 when its maquiladora came on-line in Reynosa, Tamaulipas. (The Texas plants were later

closed when the company began operations in El Salvador.) In 1970 another Sears supplier, Warwick Electronics (owned by Whirlpool), opened a maquiladora in Tijuana. Sklair, *Assembling for Development* (n. 50), describes Sears' campaign on pp. 50-52 and 131. Sklair cites James Worthy, *Shaping an American Institution: Robert E. Wood and Sears, Roebuck* (Chicago: University Press, 1984).

88. Sklair, *Assembling for Development*, 48 (see n. 50), citing a Department of State "Airgram."

89. Ibid., 48, citing Anna-Stina Ericson, "An Analysis of Mexico's Border Industrialization Program," *Monthly Labor Review* 12 (May 1970):33-40.

90. Until Mexico adopted its General Law on Ecological Equilibrium and Environmental Protection in 1988, the country's environmental policies were inadequate to deal with the pressures of industrialization and were largely unenforced. See Stephen P. Mumme, C. Richard Bath, and Valerie J. Assetto, "Political Development and Environmental Policy in Mexico," *Latin American Research Review* 23, no. 1 (1988). Despite the improved legal framework resulting from the 1988 law, inadequate regulations and enforcement remain significant obstacles to environmental protection. Mexico has not consistently enforced its strong labor standards since 1940.

91. "History of Cost per Hour in Dollars," *Twin Plant News*, Aug. 1989, 56.

92. Business International Corp., *Succeeding in the New Mexico*, 187 (see n. 52).

93. After Congress raised its objections in Oct. 1986, the Department of Commerce backed out of Expo-Maquila '86, turning responsibility over to a private public relations firm. According to the General Accounting Office, the exposition would have generated income for the government through fees paid by participants and exhibitors, and thus did not represent a net cost to taxpayers. According to congressional opponents, the GAO's calculations failed to take into account all the overhead expenses—salaries, office space, etc.—attributable to the expo. See testimony of Allan Mendelowitz to the Subcommittee on Commerce, Transportation, and Tourism of the House Committee on Energy and Commerce, 10 Dec. 1986.

94. In its first two years the coalition has launched campaigns to change the practices of more than a dozen U.S.-owned corporations, including Du Pont, Ford, General Motors, Stepan Chemical, and Zenith. Coalition for Justice in the Maquiladoras, "Summary Update on Focus Companies," (San Antonio, TX, 13 May 1992).

95. NAFTA requires Mexico to phase out the heart of the Border Industrialization Program—its duty-free provisions—by 1 Jan. 2001. "NAFTA to End Maquila Program," *El Financiero International*, 7 Sept. 1992.

96. Auto parts are subject to the general 60 percent regional-content rule under NAFTA, but they are affected indirectly by the rule of origin governing automobiles. In calculating the local content of autos, NAFTA requires that the foreign-origin portion of auto parts be considered as foreign content in the finished car, even when the parts themselves pass the regional-content test. In all other industries such foreign content in components may be "rolled up" and considered as local content if the component meets the applicable rule of origin. Medium- and large-size televisions must contain North American-made picture tubes in addition to the standard regional content to qualify for duty-free status, and computers must contain a regionally produced motherboard. The restrictions on textiles and apparel are probably the most onerous of all. Local content must be at least 80 percent, and not only the fabric used to make the apparel but even the yarn used to make the fabric must be sourced from the United States, Mexico, or Canada. See James Bovard, "NAFTA's Protectionist Bent," *Wall Street Journal*, 31 July 1992; Douglas Karmin, "Rules of Origin and the North American Free Trade Agreement," *CRS Report for Congress*, 21 Aug. 1992; and *Rules of Origin Issues Related to NAFTA and the North American Automotive Industry*, USITC Publication 2460 (Washington, DC: U.S. International Trade Commission, Nov. 1991).

97. "Wharton Econometrics Projects High Growth for Maquiladora Industry, 1993-1997," *La Jornada*, 3 Dec. 1992.

98. A number of international trade secretariats in which U.S. and Mexican unions participate are working on international codes of corporate conduct. The International Federation of Chemical, Energy and General Workers' Unions (ICEF), for example, is promoting a set of reporting requirements and restrictions to be applied to all new investments. The code would require disclosure of a corporation's investment intentions and its use and disposal of hazardous materials. It could also prohibit child labor, regulate the discharge of pollutants, set minimum standards for plant-closing notice and severance pay, and require neutrality in union-organizing efforts.

99. Williams, "Attitudes and Strategies," 61 (see n. 69).

100. Sklair, *Assembling for Development*, 135 (see n. 50), and Gene Erb, "Mexicans Fight 'Injustice' of U.S. Firms," *Des Moines Register* reprint of *Made in Mexico: The Migration of Jobs*, 1986.

101. Williams, "Attitudes and Strategies," 61 (see n. 99), and Sklair, *Assembling for Development*, 135 (see n. 50).

102. Examples from Sklair, *Assembling for Development*, 152 (see n. 50), and Williams, "Attitudes and Strategies," 62 (see n. 99). According to a longtime academic observer of labor relations on the border, "Border unions, especially those affiliated with the large national confederations, have as one of their functions that of worker control." Jorge Carrillo and Miguel Ramírez, "Maquiladoras en la frontera norte: Opinión sobre los sindicatos," *Frontera Norte IV* 2, no. 4 (July-Dec. 1990):127.

103. "A Plant Manager Admits: 'The Company Chose the Union,' " *American Labor*, no. 37 (Washington, DC: American Labor Education Center):3.

104. The AFL-CIO's role in pushing procapitalist unions in Europe, Africa, Asia, and Latin America is described in Jonathan Kwitny, *Endless Enemies: The Making of an Unfriendly World* (New York: Congdon and Weed, 1984); Hobart A. Spalding, Jr., "U.S. Labor Intervention in Latin America: The Case of the American Institute for Free Labor Development," in Roger Southall, ed., *Trade Unions and the New Industrialization of the Third World* (London: Zed Books, 1988); Beth Sims, *Workers of the World Undermined: American Labor's Role in U.S. Foreign Policy* (Boston: South End Press, 1992); and Daniel Cantor and Juliet Schor, *Tunnel Vision: Labor, the World Economy, and Central America* (Boston: South End Press, 1987). See also Tom Barry and Deb Preusch, *AIFLD In Central America* (Albuquerque: Inter-Hemispheric Education Resource Center, 1990), and Paul Garver, "Beyond the Cold War: New Directions for Labor Internationalism," *Labor Research Review* 13 (Chicago: Midwest Center for Labor Research, Fall 1989).

105. Interview with Steven Hecker of the Labor Education and Research Center at the University of Oregon, Dec. 1992.

106. Interview with a former ACTWU staff member who wished to remain anonymous, Jan. 1993. Another factor in the lack of interest on the part of union leaders was the composition of the September 19th union, according to this former staff member. "It was not only that they were an independent union, but that it was a union made up of all women and with female leadership." Because of a personal interest in the September 19th of union's organizing efforts, this staffer convinced a vice-president of ACTWU to hold a reception for workers at his own joint board down the street from the international headquarters.

107. Although diminished in intensity, the simplistic "Buy American" campaign continues to be pushed by some unions in the early 1990s. As one observer noted, such campaigns have "done little over the years to encourage U.S. workers to understand more deeply the complex process of globalization." Frances Lee Ansley, "U.S.-Mexico Free Trade from the Bottom: A Postcard from the Border," *Texas Journal of Women and the Law* 1, no. 1 (1992).

108. Ray Marshall, "Labor in a Global Economy," in Steve Hecker and Margaret Hallock, eds., *Labor in a Global Economy: Perspectives from the U.S. and Canada* (Eugene, OR: Labor Education and Research Center, 1991), 11. It is interesting to note that the trend of declining union membership in the United States is not part of a worldwide pattern. Japan's unionized work force fell from 35 percent to 28 percent from 1970 to 1986-87, but almost all other industrialized nations saw their proportions increase or stay stable over the same period. In Germany, another important international competitor, it increased from 37 percent to 43 percent.

109. The Canadian Labour Congress and several individual Canadian unions should get credit for starting the process of trinational labor organizing against NAFTA in the summer of 1990.

110. The CWA and the CWC first joined forces several years earlier in the Northern Telecom International Solidarity Coalition. This is an alliance of unions from eight countries in which Canada's Northern Telecom has a presence. Mexico, where Northern Telecom operates two nonunion plants, is not a member of the coalition. See Fred Pomeroy, "Mobilizing Across Borders: Unions and Multinational Corporations," in Hecker and Hallock, *Labor in a Global Economy* (n. 108).

111. Just when such mobilization might be deemed "necessary" by the Mexican phone workers under Hernández Juárez remains to be seen. Hernández is committed to modernizing the phone company by using foreign investment capital, and it is unlikely to risk scaring off that capital by taking any hard-line stands in support of U.S. or Canadian organizing efforts. Nor has the Mexican union shown interest in cooperating with the CWA on workplace issues, despite the latter's long experience with the opportunities and pitfalls presented by the phone technology now being installed in Mexico.

112. Quoted in David Brooks, "The Search for Counterparts," *Labor Research Review* 19 (Chicago: Midwest Center for Labor Research, 1992):83.

113. The largest labor organization that does *not* rely on government support, the Authentic Labor Front (FAT), has led Mexican opposition to NAFTA.

114. Two excellent treatments of labor's position in Mexico are Dan La Botz, *Mask of Democracy: Labor Suppression in Mexico Today* (Boston: South End Press, 1992), and Kevin J. Middlebrook, ed., *Unions, Workers, and the State in Mexico* (San Diego: Center for U.S.-Mexican Studies, 1991). For a history of Mexican labor through the austerity of the 1980s, see Kevin Middlebrook, "The Sounds of Silence: Organized Labour's Response to Economic Crisis in Mexico," *Journal of Latin American Studies* 21, no. 2 (1989):195-220, and Dan La Botz, *The Crisis of Mexican Labor* (New York: Praeger, 1988).

115. The most recent economic pact was signed Oct. 1992 and was slated to expire Dec. 1993.

116. See Kevin J. Middlebrook, "State Structures and the Politics of Union Registration in Postrevolutionary Mexico," *Comparative Politics* 23, no. 4 (July 1991):459-78.

117. Quoted in Matt Moffett, "Mexico's Union Boss, Ally of Salinas, Is a Stumbling Block in Trade Talks," *Wall Street Journal*, 5 Feb. 1991. Scheele participated in one of the most flagrant and best-known abuses of worker rights in recent decades: the repression of the Ford Democratic Workers union based at Ford's assembly plant in Cuautitlán, just north of the capital city. In Jan. 1990 thugs hired by the CTM-affiliated union hierarchy, allegedly with the assistance of Ford managers, fired on workers, wounding nine and killing one. The development of the conflict through 1992 is covered in La Botz, *Mask of Democracy*, 148-59 (see n. 114). As of late 1993 conflict continued at the plant.

118. Rebekah Greenwald, "Uncanny Silence from Crafty Carla," *NAFTA Thoughts* 1, no. 1 (Washington, DC: Development GAP, Dec. 1991).

References

119. Quoted in Matt Witt, "Labor and NAFTA," *Latin American Labor News*, no. 5 (Fall 1992), 7.

120. If approved, NAFTA will phase out 99 percent of all tariffs over ten years and eliminate remaining tariffs on politically sensitive products such as corn and beans over fifteen years.

121. Recent theoretical work on free market economies has spawned a growing school of thought that argues that even on paper, free market models do not necessarily produce optimal outcomes. This work focuses on the role of technological innovation as the driving force for economic growth. The new models have fundamental implications for free trade theory as well, and imply that free trade and investment flows between countries with similar endowments of capital and skilled labor are likely to produce greater long-term economic growth than free trade between countries with different levels of those factors. This surprising result stems from the fundamental difference between the production of goods and services and the "production" of technological innovations. In the former case, each additional unit of production "uses up" some of the finite supply of labor and, on a macroeconomic scale, capital. In the latter case, reproduction of a given technology is essentially cost-free, implying great efficiency gains from its widespread application. Joining relatively advanced countries in free trade allows for wider dissemination of technological innovations and for specialization in research and development activities. See: Gene Grossman and Elhanan Helpman, "Comparative Advantage and Long Run Growth," *American Economic Review*, Sept. 1990, 796-815; Paul A. Krugman, *Rethinking International Trade* (Cambridge, MA: MIT Press, 1990); Luis A. Rivera-Batiz and Paul M. Romer, "Economic Integration and Endogenous Growth," *Quarterly Journal of Economics* 106, no. 2 (May 1991):531-55; and Paul M. Romer, "Are Nonconvexities Important for Understanding Growth?" *American Economic Review* 80, no. 2 (May 1990):97-103.

122. A calculation by William Spriggs of the Economic Policy Institute found that even if NAFTA added two percentage points to Mexico's growth rate—a very generous estimate—the increase in U.S. exports to that country would represent only one-sixth of 1 percent of the U.S. gross domestic product.

123. Industries that stood to suffer if Mexican competitors gained equal access to their U.S. customers included textiles, apparel, footwear, leather goods, steel, glass products, automobiles, and consumer electronics. Some agricultural products, especially citrus fruits and winter vegetables, were also threatened by the prospect of free trade. This list is taken from Peter Morici, *Trade Talks with Mexico*, 60-62 (see n. 11).

124. The belief that economic development in Mexico will stem the flow of emigrants to the United States has become conventional wisdom in Washington. A number of migration experts have cast doubt on this analysis, arguing that per capita income growth actually spurs emigration among those who formerly did not have the resources to make the trek. Furthermore, tightening economic relations between the United States and Mexico both strengthens the social networks that facilitate migration and lowers the cultural barrier to migration by making the United States seem less foreign. See David C. Scott, "Free Trade and Mexican Migrants," *Christian Science Monitor*, 15 June 1992; Saskia Sassen, *The Mobility of Labor and Capital: A Study in International Investment and Labor Flow* (Cambridge: Cambridge University Press, 1988); and Saskia Sassen, "Why Migration?" *Report on the Americas* 26, no. 1 (July 1992).

125. Working step by step through bilateral and multilateral free trade agreements with eligible countries, the Enterprise for the Americas Initiative (EAI) aims eventually to have the entire Western Hemisphere joined under the same economic regime. The EAI offers access to the U.S. market and to financial and technical resources, and it provides some help with debt reduction to countries that liberalize their trade and investment policies, cut back government spending, and generally adhere to neoliberal economic prescriptions. President Bush announced the initiative in late June 1990,

just weeks after announcing the planned free trade talks with Mexico. For more on the EAI, see Betsy A. Cody and Raymond J. Ahearn, *The Enterprise for the Americas Initiative: Issues for Congress* (Washington, DC: Congressional Research Service, 30 Oct. 1992); Peter Hakim, "The Enterprise for the Americas Initiative: What Washington Wants," *Brookings Review*, Fall 1992; and "Enterprise for the Americas Initiative," interview with Xabier Gorostiaga, *Free or Fair Trade?* no. 1 (Bogotá, July 1992).

126. The United States and Mexico agreed, but with the explicit understanding that if Canadian objections significantly slowed the process, the two countries would return to a bilateral arrangement. This stance effectively eliminated Canada's bargaining power.

127. Quoted in Bruce Campbell, "Beggar Thy Neighbor," *NACLA Report on the Americas* 24, no. 6 (May 1991):23.

128. Television news media, which reach twenty times more Mexicans than all print media combined, are rarely critical of the government. All but a handful of magazines and newspapers are heavily influenced in their coverage of important issues by direct government payoffs to reporters and editors and by their dependence on the government for roughly half their advertising budgets. For several recent accounts along these lines, see Marjorie Miller, "Mexico Press Is Still Far from Free," *Los Angeles Times*, 22 Oct. 1991; David Clark Scott, "Mexico's Press Guards Its Freedom," *Christian Science Monitor*, 26 Sept. 1991; and Andres Oppenheimer, "Mexican Government Pays Media for Good Press," *Albuquerque Journal*, 2 Aug. 1992. On presidential control of the PRI and the Congress, see Andrew Reding and Christopher Whalen, *Fragile Stability: Reform and Repression in Mexico under Carlos Salinas* (New York: World Policy Institute, 1992), and Wayne A. Cornelius, Judith Gentleman, and Peter H. Smith, eds., *Mexico's Alternative Political Futures* (San Diego: Center for U.S.-Mexican Studies, 1989).

129. Larry Rohter, "Free-Trade Talks with U.S. Set Off Debate in Mexico," *New York Times*, 19 March 1990, A1.

130. Although the European process of integration has a much stronger social component than does NAFTA, it is a model only in that it points the way to greater possibilities. Many advocates of broadening NAFTA and many European activists believe that the European Community's standards were watered down out of concern for the international competitiveness of the continent's businesses. See Matthew Sanger, "Free Trade and Workers' Rights: The European Social Charter," *Briarpatch* 20, no. 7 (Saskatchewan, Sept. 1991).

131. The council was abolished in the early days of the Clinton administration, indicating that the neoliberal principles of the two previous administrations were being modified by a government that understood the need to respond to a constituency beyond the corporate sector.

132. In the wake of the Canada-U.S. Free Trade Agreement, Canada agreed to lower its pesticide standards to reach "equivalence" with U.S. regulations. See Steven Shrybman, "Trading Away the Environment," *World Policy Journal* (Winter 1991-92).

133. Soon after the Canada-U.S. Free Trade Agreement was approved, the Canadian Manufacturers Association, the Chamber of Commerce, and the powerful Business Council on National Issues called on the government to cut spending on unemployment insurance (UI). The conservative government was responsive to these demands, eliminating its $2 billion annual contribution to UI from its April 1989 budget and making several other changes that brought Canada's UI system in line with lower U.S. standards. Ecumenical Coalition for Economic Justice, *Economic Justice Report* 2, no. 3 (Oct. 1991):12.

134. Quoted in Canadian Labour Congress, *Free Trade Briefing Document*, no. 7 (Jan. 1991), 13.

135. See Shrybman, "Trading Away the Environment," (n. 132), and "Selling Canada's Environment Short: An Environmental Assessment of the First Two Years of Free Trade between Canada and the U.S." (Toronto: Canadian Environmental Law Association, 1991).

136. A free trade agreement could include a clause restricting trade with nations that failed to respect accepted standards to discourage firms from relocating outside North America to avoid regulations. There is a precedent for requiring countries to enforce minimum labor standards in order to export goods to the United States duty-free. The U.S. Trade Act of 1974 established a "Generalized System of Preferences" under which the president decides which developing countries will have duty-free access to the U.S. market, and for which products. In 1984 Congress prohibited the president from naming a country as a beneficiary "if such country has not taken or is not taking steps to afford internationally recognized worker rights to workers in the country." These measures include the right to organize and bargain collectively, standards for minimum working age, maximum hours of work, occupational safety and health, and an "acceptable" minimum wage.

137. The Bush administration, for instance, cited economic studies based on the theory of comparative advantage showing that NAFTA would produce more jobs than it would destroy—135,000 more, to be precise. Although this number represented one-ninth of 1 percent of the U.S. work force, the new jobs would be in the export sector and therefore likely to pay above-average wages, officials said. Secretary of Labor Lynn Martin, citing a study by the Institute for International Economics, gave this number in response to congressional questioning. Administration officials used the figure in public presentations throughout 1992. See Gary Clyde Hufbauer and Jeffrey J. Schott, *North American Free Trade: Issues and Recommendations* (Washington, DC: Institute for International Economics, 1992).

138. Canadian Labour Congress, *Free Trade Briefing Document* (see n. 134). Half the 250,000 jobs lost were directly attributed to free-trade-induced closings or layoffs and the other half to indirect losses in supplier industries and the service sector. The report notes that if job creation had remained at its average level of the previous five years, the Canadian economy would have gained 582,000 more jobs than it did. And the Ontario provincial government found that more than 55 percent of all layoffs in 1989 were caused by plant closings, as opposed to 22 percent of layoffs in 1982.

139. Cited by Jeff Faux and Thea Lee, "The Effect of George Bush's NAFTA on American Workers: Ladder up or Ladder down?" briefing paper prepared for the Economic Policy Institute (Washington, DC, 1992). Manufacturing employment in Canada dropped by 1 percent from 1981 to 1988.

140. For a more optimistic view of Canada's prospects under free trade with the United States, see Peter Morici, "Making the Transition to Free Trade," *Current History* (Dec. 1991). Morici argues that Canada's tight monetary policy, hard-nosed union negotiators, and overly progressive provincial governments have encouraged the exodus of manufacturing jobs.

141. See La Botz, *Mask of Democracy* (see n. 114); Matt Moffett, "Underage Laborers Fill Mexican Factories, Stir U.S. Trade Debate," *Wall Street Journal*, 8 April 1991; and the testimony of William Treanor, director of the American Youth Work Center in Washington, before the U.S. Senate Committee on Foreign Relations Subcommittee on Western Hemisphere and Peace Corps Affairs, 102nd Cong., 1st sess., 14 and 22 March and 11 April 1991, 123-28.

142. U.S. Secretary of Labor Lynn Martin and Mexican Secretary of Labor Arsenio Farrell signed a Memorandum of Understanding on 1 May 1991 and an Agreement on Labor Cooperation on 14 Sept. 1992. The latter recognized "that the two governments have the sovereign right to apply their laws in accordance with their jurisdiction and com-

petence," a recognition that was not extended in NAFTA to such questions as copyright law and farm policy.

143. George Anders, "Heading South: U.S. Companies Plan Major Moves into Mexico," *Wall Street Journal*, 24 Sept. 1992, R1. The figures were more striking when only companies with annual sales over $1 billion were included. Some 55 percent of the executives of these large corporations said they were likely to shift some production to Mexico in the coming years.

144. *The Likely Impact on the United States of a Free Trade Agreement with Mexico*, USITC Publication 2353 (Washington, DC: U.S. International Trade Commission, Feb. 1991), 2-6.

145. Testimony of William E. Spriggs of the Economic Policy Institute, before a hearing of the U.S. House of Representatives Committee on Energy and Commerce, Subcommittee on Commerce, Consumer Protection, and Competitiveness, *Free Trade Agreement*, 102nd Cong., 1st sess., 20 March and 8 and 15 May 1991, 330-31. In the ITC's updated report it found that "unskilled workers" would enjoy a wage increase of 0.011 percent. See also Jeff Faux and Richard Rothstein, "Fast Track, Fast Shuffle," briefing paper prepared for the Economic Policy Institute (Washington, DC, 1991).

146. Edward E. Leamer, "Wage Effects of a U.S.-Mexican Free Trade Agreement," paper presented at the Mexico-U.S. FTA Conference, Figure 4, Brown University, Oct. 1991.

147. *Economic Adjustment and Worker Dislocation* (see n. 3) and U.S. Congress, Office of Technology Assessment, *Technology and Structural Unemployment: Reemploying Displaced Adults*, OTA-ITE-250 (Washington, DC, Feb. 1986). The Bureau of Labor Statistics data include only "displaced" workers—defined as those who permanently lost their jobs after at least three years in the position. See also Michael Podgursky, "Estimated Losses Due to Job Displacement: Evidence from the Displaced Worker Surveys" (Washington, DC: Economic Policy Institute, April 1991).

148. Thea Lee, "Happily Never NAFTA: There's No Such Thing as a Free Trade," *Dollars & Sense*, Jan.-Feb. 1993. The Congressional Budget Office recently reviewed eleven of the most prominent academic studies of the trade pact's likely effect on the U.S. economy. Ten assumed NAFTA would have no effect on investment in the United States and one used trickle-down logic to conclude that investment here would actually increase, thanks to higher profits from moving operations to Mexico. "Estimating the Effects of NAFTA: An Assessment of the Economic Models and other Empirical Studies," *CBO Papers* (Washington, DC: Congressional Budget Office, June 1993).

149. Jeff Faux and William Spriggs, "U.S. Jobs and the Mexico Trade Proposal," briefing paper prepared for the Economic Policy Institute (Washington, DC, 1991).

150. See Timothy Koechlin and Mehrene Larudee, "The High Cost of NAFTA," *Challenge*, Sept.-Oct. 1992.

151. Some studies proceed one step further to attempt to include the possibility of changes in employment levels. They first estimate an increase in overall wage earnings, based on full employment, just as the first set of studies does. They then reason that some portion of the rise in wages paid is due to increased employment rather than just to changed wage rates. These studies are less honest than their cousins since they acknowledge the existence of unemployment but still use assumptions of full employment and perfect markets in the equations that form their models. See *Economy-wide Modeling of the Economic Implications of a FTA with Mexico and a NAFTA with Canada and Mexico*, USITC Publication 2508 (Washington, DC: U.S. International Trade Commission, May 1992).

152. Another set of studies focuses on the expected increase of exports from the United States to Mexico and uses the U.S. government's estimate that roughly twenty thousand jobs are created by every $1 billion in new exports. There are two problems with this approach. First, a large percentage—at least one-quarter—of U.S. exports to Mex-

ico go to manufacturers whose production has replaced U.S. production. In this case exports create no new jobs in suppliers—since the same products had previously been shipped to U.S. firms—and in fact indicate that jobs have been lost in the United States. The second problem stems from the fact that the trade-employment connection works both ways. If some exports create jobs, some imports must cost jobs. The studies that found employment increases caused by increased U.S. exports to Mexico often failed to explore how many jobs might be lost by dropping barriers to imports from Mexico.

153. See Louis Uchitelle, "America's Newest Industrial Belt," *New York Times*, 21 March 1993; Harley Shaiken and Stephen Herzenberg, *Automation and Global Production: Automobile Engine Production in Mexico, the United States, and Canada* (San Diego: Center for U.S.-Mexican Studies, 1987); and Shaiken, *Myths about Mexican Workers* (see n. 58).

154. Anders, "Heading South" (see n. 143).

155. Leamer, "Wage Effects" (see n. 146).

156. Quoted in Louis Uchitelle, "As Output Gains, Wages Lag," *New York Times*, 4 June 1987.

157. Trade negotiators are being forced to reconcile trade and environmental issues with respect to such international agreements as the Montreal Protocol on Substances that Deplete the Ozone Layer, the Basel Convention on the Control of the Transboundary Movement of Hazardous Wastes and Their Disposal (still awaiting the consent of the U.S. Senate), and the 1973 Convention on the International Trade in Endangered Species (CITES), which imposes strict trade controls on species that would otherwise become endangered and bans trade in species that are endangered.

158. See two excellent reports published by the Congressional Research Service: *Environment and Trade* (Washington, DC, 15 Nov. 1992) and *International Environmental Issues: Overview* (Washington, DC, 27 July 1992).

159. The convening of GATT's environmental committee was the direct result of a request by the European Free Trade Association (EFTA) reflecting rising concerns in Europe about the effect of free trade on national environmental and consumer law.

160. In the wake of unfavorable U.S. reaction, Mexico indicated that it was asking for a postponement of a final GATT ruling, but other tuna-exporting countries still pushed for a final judgment on this precedent-setting trade ruling.

161. In his 1 May 1991 Action Plan aimed at swaying environmental and, to a lesser extent, labor critics of the fast-track NAFTA negotiations, President Bush said that some environmental concerns would be treated within the agreement itself while also promising that labor and environmental issues would be addressed more thoroughly in initiatives that would run "in parallel with" the actual negotiations. The first examples of this parallel track were the Integrated Border Environmental Plan and the Environmental Review of U.S.-Mexico Environmental Issues, both released in Feb. 1992. Bush also included representatives of a few environmental organizations on the working groups that advised U.S. NAFTA negotiators but declined to create a working group specifically on the environment.

162. Reilly repeated this statement often. One instance was reported in Keith Schneider, "Trade Pact vs. Environment: Clash at a House Hearing," *New York Times*, 16 Sept. 1992, C1.

163. The Sierra Club and Public Citizen have argued that a zero tolerance regulation could be challenged under NAFTA because of the agreement's requirement that standards be consistent among the three countries.

164. Keith Schneider, "Environmentalists Fight Each Other over Trade Accord," *New York Times*, 16 Sept. 1993.

165. See Chapter Twenty of NAFTA, "Institutional Arrangements and Dispute Settlement Procedures," especially articles 2001, 2016, and 2017.

166. Lori Wallach, "The NAFTA Does Not Measure Up on the Environment and Consumer Health and Safety" (Washington, DC: Public Citizen, 1992).

167. Rather than rely on economic growth to create the needed revenues for environmental protection and enforcement, such national environmental organizations as the Sierra Club, the Natural Resources Defense Council, and the Environmental Defense Fund have proposed a variety of directed revenue-generating measures. Adhering to the "polluter should pay" principle, some propose that corporations investing in Mexico turn over a percentage of their profits to an environmental protection fund or that a "green tax" be levied on cross-border trade. It has also been suggested that countries collect pollution-control bonds from industrialists and that countervailing duties be imposed on goods manufactured using environmentally destructive practices.

168. Robert B. Zoellick of the U.S. State Department, in testimony before the U.S. Senate Committee on Foreign Relations, *North American Free Trade Agreement: Extending Fast Track Negotiating Authority*, 102nd Cong., 1st sess., 11 April 1991. The Salinas administration apparently attempted to bolster this line of attack. A major daily newspaper in Mexico, *Excelsior*, ran a front-page story on 27 Dec. 1992 reporting that a prestigious group of Mexican environmentalists had accused U.S. environmental groups of using "pseudo-environmentalist arguments" and "tendentious propaganda" to "manipulate" public opinion in opposition to free trade. Had the story been true it would have represented a significant blow to U.S. groups, which count on the support of their Mexican counterparts to overcome right-wing accusations that environmental measures are merely disguised protectionism. The organization quoted by *Excelsior*, however, immediately denied having made any such accusations. Homero Aridjis, head of the environmentalist Group of 100, accused the Mexican government of planting the story in an effort to influence the upcoming meeting between Salinas and U.S. President-elect Clinton, at which NAFTA was topic number one. Ethel Riquelme, "Argumentos seudoecologistas manipulan en EU: Los 100," *Excelsior*, 27 Dec. 1992, 1, and interview with Geoffrey Land, Border Ecology Project, 21 Jan. 1993.

169. Francisco Lara, director of the Colegio de la Frontera Norte in Nogales, Sonora, quoted in Marc Levinson, "The Green Gangs," *Newsweek*, 3 Aug. 1992.

170. See John Cavanagh et al., *Trading Freedom: How Free Trade Affects Our Lives, Work, and Environment* (San Francisco: Institute for Food and Development Policy, 1992).

171. Testimony of Lori Wallach before the U.S. House of Representatives Committee on Foreign Affairs, Subcommittee on International Economic Policy and Trade, and Subcommittee on Western Hemisphere Affairs, 9 Dec. 1991.

172. Inspired by concerns about NAFTA, coalitions of environmentalists, labor organizations, religious groups, and community activists in the United States and Mexico worked to draw the broad outlines of a pro-people and pro-environment framework for economic integration. Organizations such as the Alliance for Responsible Trade, Citizen Trade Watch Campaign, Coalition for Justice in the Maquiladoras, Fair Trade Campaign, Action Canada Network, and Mexican Action Network on Free Trade were among the most active. Most of the following discussion about ways to shape integration draws on the very important work of groups like these and the publications of analysts and activists who share their concerns. See, for example, George E. Brown, Jr., J. William Goold, and John Cavanagh, "Making Trade Fair," *World Policy Journal* (Spring 1992); Gregory, "Environment, Sustainable Development, Public Participation and the NAFTA"; Andrew A. Reding, "Bolstering Democracy in the Americas," *World Policy Journal* (Summer 1992); and Cuauhtémoc Cárdenas, "The Continental Development and Trade Initiative," speech given before the Americas Society, New York, 8 Feb. 1991.

173. Brown et al., "Making Trade Fair," 312-13 (ibid.).

174. A number of writers have criticized the economic and trade policy process for its undemocratic nature. For one of the most detailed examinations, see Gregory, "Environment, Sustainable Development, Public Participation and the NAFTA" (see n. 172).

175. For a detailed look at these issues and a potential solution, see Albert Fishlow, Sherman Robinson, and Raul Hinojosa-Ojeda, "Proposal for a North American Regional Development Bank and Adjustment Fund," presented at a conference on North American free trade sponsored by the Federal Reserve Bank of Dallas, TX, 14 June 1991.

176. Cárdenas, "The Continental Development and Trade Initiative," 6 (see n. 172).

177. Fishlow et al., "Proposal" (see n. 175). See also U.S. Congress, Office of Technology Assessment, *U.S.-Mexico Trade* (see n. 60).

178. The basic aspects of an international strategy for labor, including a code of conduct for transnational corporations, are described in Jeremy Brecher and Tim Costello, *Global Village vs. Global Pillage: A One-world Strategy for Labor* (Washington, DC: International Labor Rights Education and Research Fund, 1991). In a major setback to efforts to install such a code, an intergovernmental group at the United Nations declared in late 1992 that no consensus was possible on provisions of the code. The group's conclusions marked the end of a thirteen-year process to create and install the code under UN auspices.

179. See Reding, "Bolstering Democracy in the Americas" (n. 172); Peter A. Schey, "North American Economic Integration: A Multilateral Approach to Migration and the Human Rights of Migrant Workers," paper presented at the 16th Annual Conference on Immigration and Naturalization at the University of Texas at Austin School of Law, San Antonio, TX, 17-18 Sept. 1992; and Minnesota Advocates for Human Rights, "No Double Standards in International Law: Linkage of NAFTA with Hemispheric System of Human Rights Enforcement Is Needed" (Minneapolis, 1992).

180. Schey, "North American Economic Integration," 6 (ibid.).

181. Among the many authors or organizations that have explored the idea of a social charter that would parallel or be contained within a free trade agreement are: U.S. Congress, Office of Technology Assessment, *U.S.-Mexico Trade*, 48-50 (see n. 60); Brown et al., "Making Trade Fair" (see n. 172); Seminario Permanente de Estudios Chicanos y de Fronteras, "Proposal for a Tri-National Declaration of Human Rights" (Mexico, D.F., 1992); J.M. Servais, "The Social Clause in Trade Agreements: Wishful Thinking or an Instrument of Social Progress?" *International Labour Review* 128, no. 4 (1989); Gijsbert van Liemt, "Minimum Labour Standards and International Trade: Would a Social Clause Work?" *International Labour Review* 128, no. 4 (1989); and Sanger, "Free Trade and Workers' Rights" (see n. 130).

182. U.S. Congress, Office of Technology Assessment, *U.S.-Mexico Trade*, 48 (see n. 60).

183. See the proposals in Proyecto Fronterizo de Educación Ambiental and Border Ecology Project, "The North American Free Trade Agreement" (Bisbee, AZ), and Gregory, "Environment, Sustainable Development, Public Participation and the NAFTA" (see n. 172).

184. This idea was proposed Oct. 1992 in an electronic forum on NAFTA by Robert W. Benson, a law professor at the Loyola Law School in Los Angeles, CA. He described the initiative as part of a "Clean Hands Amendment for NAFTA" that would also include a NAFTA Human Rights Commission to oversee elections and hear complaints about human rights abuses.

Resources

The organizations listed below are among the most active in the ongoing debate over economic integration and in efforts to develop cross-border links among labor groups. For a more complete listing, see the Resource Center's *Cross-Border Links: A Directory of Organizations in Canada, Mexico, and the United States* (1992) or consult the Resource Center's Cross-Border Clearinghouse, a database containing more than a thousand individual and organizational contacts involved in various aspects of U.S.-Mexico relations.

Amalgamated Clothing and Textile Workers Union (ACTWU)
15 Union Square
New York, NY 10003-3377
Phone: (212) 242-0700
Contact: Ron Blackwell

American Federation of Labor-Congress of Industrial Organizations (AFL-CIO)
815 16th St. NW
Washington, DC 20006
Phone: (202) 637-5187
Fax: (202) 637-5058
Contact: Ed Feigen

American Labor Education Center (ALEC)
2000 P St. NW #300
Washington, DC 20036
Phone: (202) 828-5170
Fax: (202) 828-5173
Email: ALEC (PeaceNet)

Center for U.S.-Mexican Studies
University of California, San Diego
La Jolla, CA 92093-0510
Phone: (619) 534-4503
Fax: (619) 534-6447

Centro de Investigación Laboral y Asesoría (CILAS)
Dr. Liceaga 180 A-5, Desp. 1001, Col. Doctores
México, D.F.
Teléfono: (5) 5-78-72-97
Fax: (5) 5-78-72-97
Contacto: Luis Bueno Rodríguez, Director

Citizens' Trade Campaign
215 Pennsylvania Ave. SE
Washington, DC 20003
Phone: (202) 554-1102
Fax: (202) 554-1654
Contact: Jim Joontz or Scott Paul

Coalition for Justice in the Maquiladoras
530 Bandera Rd.
San Antonio, TX 78228
Phone: (512) 735-4988
Fax: (512) 735-2615
Contact: Susan Mika

Colegio de la Frontera Norte (COLEF)
Blvd. Abelardo L. Rodríguez 21, Zona del Río
Tijuana, B.C. 22320
Mailing address in the United States: PO Box L, Chula Vista, CA 92912
Phone: (66) 30-04-11
Fax: (66) 30-00-50
Contact: Dr. Jorge Carrillo V., Director General Académico

Communications Workers of America
501 3rd St. NW
Washington, DC 20001-2797
Phone: (202) 434-1185
Fax: (202) 434-1201
Contact: Steve Abrecht, Research Economist

Confederación de Trabajadores Mexicanos (CTM)
Vallarta 8, Col. Tabacalera
México, D.F. 06470
Phone: (5) 7-05-10-91
Contact: Tomás Martínez

Despacho Obrero
Isaac Newton 936 Col. Del Futuro
Ciudad Juárez, Chih.
Phone: (16) 18-43-77
Contact: Gustavo de la Rosa

Development GAP (Group for Alternative Policies)
1400 I St. NW #520
Washington, DC 20005
Phone: (202) 898-1566
Fax: (202) 898-1612
Email: dgap@igc.apc.org
Contact: Karen Hansen-Kuhn

Economic Policy Institute
1730 Rhode Island Ave. NW #200
Washington, DC 20036
Phone: (202) 775-8810
Fax: (202) 775-0819
Contact: Thea Lee

Equipo Pueblo
Francisco Field Jurado 51, Col. Independencia
México, D.F. 03630
Mailing Address: A.P. 27-467 México, D.F. 06760
Phone: (5) 5-39-00-15/55
Fax: (5) 6-72-74-53
Email: pueblo@igc.apc.org
Contact: Carlos Heredia

Fair Trade Campaign
Western Regional Office
425 Mississippi St.
San Francisco, CA 94107
Phone: (415) 826-6314
Fax: (415) 826-5303
Contact: Craig Merrilees

Farm Labor Organizing Committee (FLOC)
507 S. Saint Clair
Toledo, OH 43602
Phone: (419) 243-3456
Fax: (419) 243-5655
Contact: Baldemar Velásquez

Federation for Industrial Retention and Renewal (FIRR)
3411 W. Diversey #10
Chicago, IL 60647
Phone: (312) 252-7676
Fax: (312) 278-5918
Contact: Jim Benn, Executive Director

Frente Auténtico del Trabajo (FAT)
Godard 20, Col. Guadalupe Victoria
México, D.F. 07790
Phone: (5) 5-56-93-75/14
Fax: (5) 5-56-93-16
Email: rmalc@igc.apc.org
Contact: Bertha E. Luján

Institute for Agriculture & Trade Policy
1313 5th St. SE #303
Minneapolis, MN 55414-1546
Phone: (612) 379-5980
Fax: (612) 379-5982
Email: iatp@igc.apc.org
Contact: Michelle Thom

International Labor Rights Education & Research Fund
PO Box 74
100 Maryland Ave. NE
Washington, DC 20002
Phone: (202) 544-7198
Fax: (202) 543-5999
Email: laborrights@igc.apc.org
Contact: Pharis Harvey

International Ladies' Garment Workers' Union (ILGWU)
1710 Broadway
New York, NY 10019
Phone: (212) 265-7000
Fax: (212) 489-6796
Contact: Jeff Hermanson

Labor Notes
7435 Michigan Ave.
Detroit, MI 48210
Phone: (313) 842-6262
Fax: (313) 842 0227
Email: labornotes@igc.apc.org
Contact: Mary McGinn

Mexico-U.S. Diálogos
870 President St.
Brooklyn, NY 11215
Phone: (718) 230-3628
Fax: (718) 399-0312
Contact: David Brooks

Midwest Center for Labor Research
3411 Diversey Ave. #10
Chicago, IL 60647
Phone: (312) 278-5418
Contact: Karen May

Mujer a Mujer
A.P. 24-553, Col. Roma
México, D.F. 06701
Mailing address in the U.S.: PO Box 12322, San Antonio, TX 78212
Phone: (5) 2-07-08-34
Fax: (5) 5-84-10-68
Email: mam@igc.apc.org
Contact: Mercedes López

Mujeres en Acción Sindical (MAS)
Aragón 122, Col. Los Alamos
México D.F. 03400
Phone: (5) 5-19-80-48
Contact: Patricia Mercado

North American Worker-to-Worker Newtwork
PO Box 1993
Rocky Mount, NC 27802
Phone: (919) 985-1957
Fax: (919) 985-2052
Contact: Jacki Van Anda

PROFMEX-Consortium for Research on Mexico
UCLA Program on Mexico
Los Angeles, CA 90024
Phone: (310) 454-8812
Fax: (310) 454-3109
Contact: George Baker, Executive Secretary

Programa de Educación Laboral y Sindical, SEMPO
Valladolid 33 Col. Roma
México, D.F. 05700
Phone: (5) 2-07-80-19/5-25-22-36
Fax: (5) 5-84-38-95
Contact: José Antonio Vital Galicia

Public Citizen
215 Pennsylvania Ave. SE
Washington, DC 20003
Phone: (202) 546-4996
Fax: (202) 547-7392
Contact: Lori Wallach

Red Mexicana de Acción Frente al Libre Comercio (RMALC)
Godard 20, Col. Guadalupe Victoria
México, D.F. 07790
Phone: (5) 5-56-93-75/14
Fax: (5) 5-56-93-16
Email: rmalc@igc.apc.org
Contact: Manuel García Urrutia

Sindicato de Telefonistas de la República Mexicana (STRM)
Villalongín 50, Col. Cuautémoc
México, D.F. 06500
Phone: (5) 5-66-12-27 / 46-45-05
Contact: Francisco Hernández Juárez, Secretary General

Sindicato Mexicano de Electricistas (SME)
Antonio Caso 45, Col. San Rafael
Mailing address: A.P. 10439
México, D.F. 06470
Phone: (5) 5-35-03-86
Contact: Antonio Durán

Sindicato Nacional de Trabajadores de la Industria de la Costura, 19 Septiembre
San Antonio Abad 151, Col. Obrera
Mailing address: A.P. M-10578, Col. Centro
México, D.F. 06200
Phone: (5) 7-41-33-07
Contact: Gloria Juandiego Monzón

Teamsters Union
25 Louisiana NW
Washington, DC 20001
Phone: (202) 624-6800
Contact: Matt Witt

United Electrical, Radio, and Machine Workers of America (UE)
1800 Diagonal Rd., #600
Alexandria, VA 22314
Phone: (703) 684-3123
Contact: Bob Kingsley

Index

About the Authors

Harry Browne is a research associate at the Inter-Hemispheric Education Resource Center. He is a co-author of *The Great Divide: The Challenge of U.S.-Mexico Relations in the 1990s* (Grove Press, forthcoming) and of *Runaway America: U.S. Jobs and Factories on the Move* (Resource Center Press, 1993). He received his Master's of Pacific International Affairs from the Graduate School of International Relations and Pacific Studies at the University of California, San Diego.

Beth Sims, a research associate at the Inter-Hemispheric Education Resource Center, is the author, co-author, or contributor to several books, including *The Great Divide: The Challenge of U.S.-Mexico Relations in the 1990s*, *Runaway America: U.S. Jobs and Factories on the Move*, *Workers of the World Undermined: American Labor's Role in U.S. Foreign Policy* (South End Press, 1992), and *Mexico: A Country Guide* (Resource Center, 1992). She received her Master's in Political Science from the University of New Mexico.

Tom Barry has been a senior analyst at the Inter-Hemispheric Education Resource Center since its founding in 1979. He is a co-author of *The Great Divide: The Challenge of U.S.-Mexico Relations in the 1990s* and is the author or co-author of all the books in the Resource Center's *Country Guide* series. He is the author of *Central America Inside Out* (Grove Weidenfeld, 1991), co-author of *Feeding the Crisis* (University of Nebraska Press, 1991), and author of *Roots of Rebellion* (South End Press, 1986).

Resource Center Press

Resource Center Press is the imprint of the Inter-Hemispheric Education Resource Center, a private, non-profit, research and policy institute located in Albuquerque, New Mexico. Founded in 1979, the Resource Center produces books, policy reports, audiovisuals, and other educational materials about U.S. foreign policy, as well as sponsoring popular education projects. For more information and a catalog of publications, please write to the Resource Center, Box 4506, Albuquerque, New Mexico 87196.

Board of Directors

Forthcoming from Grove Press, April 1994

The Great Divide

The Challenge of U.S.-Mexico Relations in the 1990s

Tom Barry, Harry Browne, and Beth Sims

"All international borders are at once fascinating and disconcerting . . . But it is not the contrasting cultures . . . that [make] crossing the U.S.-Mexico line so shocking . . . it is the experience of passing so rapidly between economic worlds.**"** — *excerpt*

The Great Divide is an in-depth examination of the U.S.-Mexico relationship—one that has often been volatile, characterized by prejudice, imperialism, and violence, and only recently by cooperation and mutual dependence. This precarious harmony is threatened by the potentially problematic ramifications of the North American Free Trade Agreement, which, if passed, promises to change permanently the nature of the relationship.

Bound as the U.S. and Mexico are by trade, debt, immigration, and the drug war, the economic and social issues that face both countries play out most visibly along the border. Nine thousand people a day cross illegally into the U.S. through the borderlands; 2,000 maquiladora factories spread across the borderlands employ nearly 500,000 Mexicans and yet are subject to virtually no labor or environmental laws; 50 percent of the cocaine and 75 percent of the marijuana smuggled into the U.S. comes through the borderlands; and the pollution in the area is so bad that a section of the Nogales Wash, a borderlands river, recently exploded.

This is another book in the Grove Press series which includes *The Central America Fact Book* and *Central America Inside Out*.

Mexico: A Country Guide

*The Essential Source on Mexican Society,
Economy, and Politics*

Edited by Tom Barry

One of our best sellers, *Mexico: A Country Guide* is the only comprehensive book about Mexican society, politics, and economy in the 1990s—an invaluable resource for students, academics, and anyone interested in the interrelationship between our two countries. Includes photos, tables and charts, references, and index.

"Easily the best source book on contemporary Mexican society." – Choice: Current Reviews for College Libraries

ISBN: 0-911213-35-X
Paperback, 401 pages, 1992.
For U.S. orders: **Send $14.95 plus $3.00 shipping
and handling to: Resource Center,
Box 4506, Albuquerque, NM 87196 USA**
For U.K. orders: **Send £11.50 to Latin America Bureau, 1
Amwell Street, London EC1R 1UL**

BorderLines

A quarterly from the Resource Center focusing on border issues

This quarterly is an extension of the Resource Center's work on its Cross-Border Links project. It examines the dynamics of cross-border relations, highlighting the problems and successes of popular organizations and government agencies in resolving common issues. It also offers investigative reporting and timely policy analysis about Mexico-U.S. relations.

**U.S. subscriptions: $10/year, $17/2 years
Foreign subscriptions: $15/year, $27/2 years**

Prices subject to change.

Resource Center
Box 4506 / Albuquerque, NM 87196 USA
(505) 842-8288

The U.S.-Mexico Series

The Challenge of Cross-Border Environmentalism:
The U.S.-Mexico Case

Few predicted the clout environmentalists now have in international trade discussions. Suddenly, environmental issues have become central to the rapidly evolving relationship between the United States and Mexico. *The Challenge of Cross-Border Environmentalism* explores diverse environmental issues—including cross-border air and water contamination, pesticides, pollution-haven investment, maquiladora wastes, sharing of water resources, and impacts of liberalized trade—and examines how governments and citizen groups are responding to new environmental challenges. The book, copublished by the Resource Center Press and the Border Ecology Project, focuses on conditions in the U.S.-Mexico borderlands where many of these problems and challenges are most apparent.

No. 1 in the series. ISBN: 0-911213-45-7. 121 pages, paperback, $9.95

On Foreign Soil: Government Programs in U.S.-Mexico Relations

Disagreements and misunderstandings have traditionally characterized the U.S.-Mexico relationship. Since the mid-1980s, however, the two governments have increasingly seen eye to eye on issues ranging from economics to international affairs. Similar economy policy agendas—characterized by neoliberal policies and free trade initiatives—are the foundation of this new mutual understanding. But simmering beneath the improved relations are such intractable issues as immigration, labor mobility, narcotrafficking, economic disparities, and asymmetric trading and investment power. *On Foreign Soil* breaks new ground in examining current U.S.-Mexico foreign relations, while providing an investigative look at the government programs that characterize this fragile new partnership.

No. 2 in the series. ISBN: 0-911213-44-9. 84 pages, paperback, $9.95

Crossing the Line:
Immigrants, Economic Integration, and Drug Enforcement on the
U.S.-Mexico Border

Crossing the Line takes a close and current look at the U.S.-Mexico borderlands. It is along a common border that many of the challenges that face the two nations are most acutely felt. The society and economy of the borderlands reflect historic tensions and divisions between the two nations. At the same time, the increasing interdependence of the neighboring countries is most apparent in the border region. The book looks closely at the cross-border problems presented by the northward migration stream, the maquila economy, the booming narcotics trade, and the infrastructure crisis—problems that extend beyond the borderlands to the heart of U.S.-Mexico relations.

No. 3 in the series. ISBN: 0-911213-46-5. 146 pages, paperback, $9.95

In the U.S.: Include $3.00 shipping and handling for the first book, 50¢ for each additional.
In the U.K.: Include $4.00 shipping and handling for the first book, $1.50 for each additional. Orders sent by surface book rate.
Prices subject to change.

Resource Center
Box 4506 / Albuquerque, NM 87196 USA
(505) 842-8288

On The Line

Life on the US-Mexican Border

Augusta Dwyer

The border between Mexico and the US is a unique meeting point of the First and Third Worlds. For decades it has been a source of tension between Washington and Mexico City, as millions of impoverished Mexicans defy the US Border Patrol and head for the promised lands of California and other Southern States.

For 30 years a restricted version of the North American Free Trade Agreement (NAFTA) has allowed US industries to set up cheap labour plants along the border. The 2,000 maquiladora factories are Mexico's fastest growing industrial sector, providing nearly 500,000 low wage jobs, most of them for young women.

In *On The Line*, Augusta Dwyer journeys along the length of the border, uncovering the stories of dozens of ordinary Mexicans— maquila workers, illegal migrants and environmental activists. She journeys through the crowded, dirty border cities of Ciudad Juárez and Tijuana and reveals the costs of free trade, and what Mexicans are doing to try to end their exploitation and the destruction of their environment.

200 pages, 1994. £10.00. ISBN 0 906156 84 X.

The above prices are for paperback editions and include post and packing. Write for a free LAB Books catalogue to:

Latin America Bureau
1 Amwell Street
London EC1R 1UL